# THE GOD I KNOW

*Donna Varnes*
1 Cor 2:1-5

# The God I Know

DONNA VARNES

iUniverse LLC
Bloomington

# THE GOD I KNOW

*Copyright © 2014 Donna Varnes.*

*All rights reserved. No part of this book may be used or reproduced by any means, graphic, electronic, or mechanical, including photocopying, recording, taping or by any information storage retrieval system without the written permission of the publisher except in the case of brief quotations embodied in critical articles and reviews.*

*iUniverse books may be ordered through booksellers or by contacting:*

*iUniverse LLC*
*1663 Liberty Drive*
*Bloomington, IN 47403*
*www.iuniverse.com*
*1-800-Authors (1-800-288-4677)*

*Because of the dynamic nature of the Internet, any web addresses or links contained in this book may have changed since publication and may no longer be valid. The views expressed in this work are solely those of the author and do not necessarily reflect the views of the publisher, and the publisher hereby disclaims any responsibility for them.*

*Any people depicted in stock imagery provided by Thinkstock are models, and such images are being used for illustrative purposes only. Certain stock imagery © Thinkstock.*

*ISBN: 978-1-4917-1833-9 (sc)*
*ISBN: 978-1-4917-1834-6 (e)*

*Printed in the United States of America.*

*iUniverse rev. date: 12/18/2013*

## Contents

INTRODUCTION.................................................................. vii

| | | | |
|---|---|---|---|
| 1. | 1965 | SAVED BECAUSE OF A LITTLE BOY........ | 1 |
| 2. | 1972 | THE LOST TICKET..................................... | 6 |
| 3. | 1972 | BLESSED SEEDS........................................ | 10 |
| 4. | 1972 | THE SMOKING ENGINE ........................... | 13 |
| 5. | 1973 | THE NO FALLING PRAYER........................ | 17 |
| 6. | 1973 | STRANGE DOUBLE HEALING................... | 20 |
| 7. | 1973 | THE SWEETHEARTS BANQUET ................ | 23 |
| 8. | 1974 | THE SALESMAN ...................................... | 25 |
| 9. | 1974 | THE TERRIBLE COUGH ........................... | 28 |
| 10. | 1974 | FEEDING THE ELEVEN............................. | 32 |
| 11. | 1974 | THE EAR INFECTION ............................... | 34 |
| 12. | 1975 | THE HEADACHE PRAYER ........................ | 37 |
| 13. | 1976 | KERRY GETS RAN OVER ......................... | 40 |
| 14. | 1976 | THE FROG PRAYER.................................. | 44 |
| 15. | 1977 | IS THIS REGULAR FOOD OR DO WE HAVE TO PRAY OVER IT?......... | 47 |
| 16. | 1977 | THE MISSING FINGER ............................. | 50 |
| 17. | 1977 | ACCIDENTS, TORNADOS AND THE RED SPORTS CAR............................................ | 53 |
| 18. | 1978 | THE SONG GOD GAVE AND TOOK AWAY.......... | 55 |
| 19. | 1978 | THE LITTLE HOTDOG PRAYER ................ | 59 |
| 20. | 1978 | STRETCHING THE LAST GALLON ............ | 62 |
| 21. | 1980 | HE SET ME IN A LARGE PLACE ............... | 66 |
| 22. | 1981 | OUR DAILY BREAD ISN'T PRACTICAL LORD.... | 69 |

| # | Year | Title | Page |
|---|---|---|---|
| 23. | 1982 | THE DIAPER PRAYER | 73 |
| 24. | 1983 | THE PRIME RIB STORY | 76 |
| 25. | 1985 | THE MILK PRAYER | 79 |
| 26. | 1985 | THE BLUE STATION WAGON | 82 |
| 27. | 1990 | THE MIRACLE OF THE STUFF | 85 |
| 28. | 1990 | HERE—WILL THIS COVER IT? | 88 |
| 29. | 1998 | GOD SPEAKS | 92 |
| 30. | 1998 | THE HEAVY WEIGHT | 95 |
| 31. | 1999 | ZIG-ZAGGING ON THE GLENNALLEN | 97 |
| 32. | 2000 | THE HAIL PRAYER | 100 |
| 33. | 2000 | THE FUR COAT INCIDENT | 103 |
| 34. | 2001 | THE GREAT PHYCIAN MAKES A NIGHT CALL | 106 |
| 35. | 2001 | DEGENREATIVE DISC DISEASE REVERSED | 110 |
| 36. | 2006 | JEFF'S DOG | 114 |
| 37. | 2006 | LEARNING SPIRITUAL WARFARE | 118 |
| 38. | 2006 | THE COCKROACH PRAYER | 124 |
| 39. | 2006 | THE CHRISTMAS DRESS | 127 |
| 40. | 2007 | THE ANGEL SURPRISE | 131 |
| 41. | 2007 | MY TWENTY DOLLAR ALLOWANCE FROM THE LORD | 134 |
| 42. | 2008 | SLEEPING IN TORNADO ALLEY | 137 |
| 43. | 2008 | THE WEDDING BLESSING | 140 |
| 44. | 2008 | THE FORGOTTEN PURSE | 143 |
| 45. | 2009 | THE FORGOTTEN KEYS | 145 |
| 46. | 2009 | THE TEETH PRAYER | 148 |
| 47. | 2009 | THE PRAYING OVER TIRES | 151 |
| 48. | 2009 | KEVIN'S HARROWING EXPERIENCE | 154 |
| 49. | 2009 | AMANDA'S WRECK | 158 |

CONCLUSION ............................................................................. 161

# INTRODUCTION

Write this into a permanent record to be remembered forever.
Exodus 17:14

God told me not to worry about promoting my books and writings, but to get back to doing what He told me to do—write. Quite a few years ago I got the idea to write a book to pass down to my children and grandchildren. I wanted to tell them that the reason I was convinced beyond a shadow of a doubt that there was a God and that He was involved in the world and our lives and that He loved us, was not because of something I read in a book or heard someone give a convincing talk on but because God himself has proved himself to me over and over in my life.

I wanted to leave an account of the many miracles, prayer answers and divine interventions that have occurred in the lives of my own family over the years. The part that is so amazing is not that he still does miracles and answers prayers but that He will do so for ordinary people living ordinary lives and on a daily basis. You don't have to be somebody special. You don't have to "earn" his love or "deserve" your prayer answer. Matthew 9:29 says, "and Jesus said unto them . . . According to your faith be it unto you."

God's advice to those who feel like they don't have enough faith is found in Romans 10:17 "So then faith cometh by hearing, and hearing by the word of God." Get into the word—study it—apply it—obey it. And all the while keep praying about everything and God will do the rest. Your faith will grow. If we truly believed that what we prayed would come to pass, we would have no problem obeying the verse that says, "Pray without ceasing." 1 Thessalonians 5:17

*Donna Varnes*

    I also want to clarify something. You might get the impression by hearing the testimonies I am about to share that I pray mostly for myself and my family, which is not true. We have a list of over 150 people and ministries that we pray for weekly. It is just that I feel the Lord has impressed me to share MY personal testimony, and let others share theirs.

    My hope is that as you read MY testimonies that you will be filled with hope and faith yourself and begin to reach out to our Heavenly Father who already has his hands stretched out towards you.

Now also when I am old and
grey-headed O God,
forsake me not,
until I have shown thy
strength unto this
generation and thy power
to everyone that is to come
Psalms 71:1

# SAVED BECAUSE OF A LITTLE BOY

### El Cajon, California 1965

I was staying with my dad during the summer of 1965. He was attending a Southern Baptist Church which was sponsoring a summer camp, so he paid my way to go.

Every day they had crafts and various activities as well as a chapel service in the afternoon and evening. Every day during chapel, they gave the invitation to "get saved."

I watched. This is what I always did. For as far back as I could remember I had always been a spectator of life. I watched the kids in my school play games, I watched others play sports. I watched life go on around me but I rarely participated, especially in group activities. I never felt part of the people around me—it was "me" and "them"—not "us". So it never occurred to me to go forward with "them", even though I was in agreement that "they" should.

But as I was standing in the pew singing, the young boy next to me, who I had never spoken too, asked me a question. "Have you ever gone forward and given your life to Christ?"

Startled, I replied, "no." It seemed a novel thought to me.

"Don't you think you should?"

I pondered that for a moment as I did everything and came to a conclusion. "Yes!" So I moved past him and went forward. A lady counselor had me repeat after her the sinner's prayer: "Lord I believe you are the Son of God and that you died for my sins. I ask you to forgive me for my sins and save me." Then she quoted the verse, Romans 10:9 "if thou shalt confess with thy mouth the Lord Jesus, and shalt believe in thine heart that God hath raised him from the dead, thou shalt be saved." Then she told me I needed to tell someone I had gotten saved.

When I went back to the bunkhouse I shared with about eight other girls and got out my notebook and wrote a note to my mom in Montana and my dad in California and told them I had just gotten "saved" at camp. Then I mailed them off. *There*, I thought, *I got that taken care of.*

As strange as it sounds now, I thought that was all there was to the Christian life. I did not know it was a growing relationship with the one who had saved me. I did not know I should do any other thing. No one told me about making Jesus Lord of my life and asking him about His plans and purposes for me. No one told me I should read the Bible so it could teach and guide me through life. No one told me if I would pray God would hear and answer my prayers. So I went on as I was before for several years.

However God knew I was sincere in my decision. He also knew what I didn't know, and He was okay with that. He accepted my simple confession of faith and saw me take that step towards Him. Regardless of what I felt or didn't feel or what I did or didn't do—God wrote my name in His book of life that day.

Then He set about to teach me, and to transform me. It has been a lifelong journey and it won't ever end. He has always known me and everything about me, but now I am getting to know Him and everything about Him. As I do, my life becomes sweeter and better. I have put away my fears and worries as I learn by experience how faithful and dependable God is. Everything in this confusing world starts to make sense as you read His love letter to us and get to know His character, His power, and His great love for "US."

Yes, I emphasize "us" because God has also shown me that He has made us all to think and act and do things differently, not to separate and isolate us, but because He has different purposes and plans for each of us. He did not use a cookie cutter in designing us. But like a rare piece of art, He formed each one of us in a unique manner pleasing to him. We are all born His perfect creation. He desires us to live in unity and to respect and honor one another. It is only sin that mars us. Still, He is able to restore us no matter how damaged our lives have become.

"Therefore if any man be in Christ,
he is a new creature:
old things are passed away;
behold, all things are
become new."
I Corinthians 5:17

*Donna Varnes*

## NOTE

You might notice that there is quite a gap of time between the year I got saved and my first prayer testimony. It is not because I can't look back now and see ways that God intervened or blessed in my life, as He certainly did. But during those years I was not praying. I didn't know that I was supposed to be communicating with God on a daily basis, and I certainly didn't know he wanted to communicate with me. When good things happened I did not attribute them to God nor give him the glory.

Just as an infant does not fully appreciate and recognize that in their early years they owe their very existence and survival to their mother, I was oblivious to all that God was doing behind the scenes even before I got around to praying or talking to God.

VERILY, VERILY, I SAY UNTO YOU
HE THAT HEARETH MY WORD,
AND BELIEVETH ON HIM
THAT SENT ME, HATH
EVERLASTING LIFE, AND SHALL
NOT COME INTO
CONDEMNATION;
BUT IS PASSED FROM
DEATH UNTO LIFE.
JOHN 5:24

# THE LOST TICKET

### Seattle, Washington 1972

We were sitting in our living room one evening when we heard a commotion outside. Ed looked and saw that some bigger boys had surrounded a young girl and were taunting her.

Ed ran outside and made the boys leave. Then he asked the girl where she lived and offered to give her a ride home on his motorcycle. She gratefully accepted, but the problem was Ed only had one helmet. He decided to put the helmet on her and took her home.

On the way a policemen stopped him and gave him a ticket for riding without a helmet. So when Ed got home he showed me the $50 ticket. It seemed pretty unfair, when he was just trying to make sure the girl got home safely, but what could we do.

The other problem was we did not have $50 and didn't know when we would. Ed was attending college and was only working part time. So the fine kept getting put off.

A few months later we were driving on the freeway in Seattle when Ed got pulled over because his brake lights weren't working. For some reason the officer asked if Ed had any other tickets, perhaps referring to a fix-it ticket on the brakes. Ed replied, "Yes I have a ticket for driving a motorcycle without a helmet."

"One that is not paid?" he asked.

"Right."

"How long ago did you get the ticket?" he asked.

"Oh, it's been several months."

"Then there is probably a warrant out for your arrest," he said with sudden interest. Turning to me he said, "You might have to drive home." And he turned back to his car to run a check on it.

I immediately started praying. It wasn't just that we would have another fine to pay or that they might even lock up Ed that had me in a panic—what scared me the most was the prospect of having to drive on the free-way and find my way home. I hated driving in city traffic and couldn't find my way anywhere.

"Why did you have to mention the ticket?" I complained.

"Because he asked—and besides, they always check those sort of things anyway."

The police officer took a long time in his patrol car, while I waited nervously in the car begging God to intervene and give us mercy.

Finally the cop came back. "Well, we could not find any record of you EVER having a ticket. So I am just going to write you up a warning this time, but get those brake lights fixed right away. You are free to go."

Apparently the Lord didn't think it was right to get a ticket for helping a little girl get home safely either. It is nice to have a Father with connections.

"And mercy rejoices against judgement."

James 2:13

Our family in 1972: Kevin (6), Ed, Kandi (4 months), Donna, Kim (4)

# BLESSED SEEDS

### Seattle, Washington 1972

Ed was attending the spring quarter at Puget Sound College of the Bible in Seattle. He found a job as a security guard. We were living in low income housing in White Center but to us it was great: The brick duplex was freshly painted and cleaned; nothing was in need of repair.

Six-year-old Kevin had his own bedroom for the first time since it was not acceptable to the state for brothers and sisters to share a room. Therefore our four year old daughter, Kim and baby Kandi had their own room too, and there was furniture provided for every room. It was the height of luxury for us and since the rent was based on our income we only paid $35 a month! We were oblivious to the crime rate and drug dealing in the area—and never had any major problems there—again a testament to God's watch care.

We found a nearby Christian church to attend and all was well. One day Kevin and Kim came out of Sunday school each holding a Styrofoam cup of dirt. They had planted some seeds in their cups and the teacher told them that if they took good care of them they would have some seedlings in about ten days. When we got home I instructed them to put the cups in our sunniest windowsill.

They were very conscientious and I didn't have to remind them to water their seeds. This was especially true of Kim who checked on her pot constantly looking for signs of growth. I smiled when I heard Kim praying for her seeds to hurry up and grow.

However when Kevin heard her praying again for her seeds he corrected her. "You're supposed to pray for people not your seeds!"

"Yes I can!" Kim insisted.

Of course they both looked at me to settle the dispute. "She can pray for her seeds if she wants too. It can't hurt." So Kim continued to pray for her seeds but Kevin thought it was silly.

God expressed his own opinion when Kim's seedlings emerged in five days instead of ten. Kevin's seeds never sprouted at all.

Whosoever therefore shall humble himself as this little child, the same is greatest in the kingdom of heaven

Matthew 18:4

# THE SMOKING ENGINE

### Seattle, WA to Libby, Montana 1973

When the 1973 spring quarter ended at Puget Sound College of the Bible, we loaded up all our things and headed to Montana so Ed could work on the Libby Dam for the summer. We had our three young children in the back of our station wagon and I was expecting our fourth.

We were still a couple hundred miles away when the car started acting up. We of course started praying. The engine started making a squealing sound so we tried to drown it out by singing praise choruses to the Lord. It would stop squealing and we would relax for a bit and then it would start up again and scare us and we would all start praying and singing some more. Again it stopped and we all started smiling.

Then the engine light came on. As always, we had just enough gas money to make it to his sister Irene's house in Libby. Even a minor repair was not in our budget—so we kept up the prayer and singing as it coughed, sputtered and smoked.

"PLEASE! PLEASE! PLEASE LORD—just help us make it all the way to Irene and Al's house," I pleaded. All the kids were praying right along with us, and every mile post we passed became another victory.

We were never as relieved as when we pulled into their driveway. At just that moment the car sputtered one last time and died. Ed tried restarting it but the engine had locked up there in the driveway.

We looked at each other and smiled, "I guess we DID just ask the Lord to get us to Irene's house—and that's exactly what he did," Ed said.

When we went through our mail that had been stacking up at Irene's in our absence, we came across an unexpected check. God is so timely! We used it to get the parts to rebuild the engine and Ed's brother-in-law

*Donna Varnes*

Al helped him do the work. Ed was able to carpool with Al till we had our vehicle up and running again.

By then we found a large two story three bedroom house we could rent for $175 right behind the Rosauer's grocery store—another of God's provisions.

That the generation to come might know them, (*the works of God*) the children who would be born, that they may arise and declare them to their children, that they may set their hope in God, and not forget the works of God, but keep his commandments.

Psalms 78:6-7

Kandi sitting on her baby brother Kerry
They are one year and 13 days apart

# THE NO FALLING PRAYER

Seattle, Washington, 1973

When we returned to Seattle, Washington for the next quarter at Puget Sound College of the Bible, we again took with us only what would fit in our station wagon. Since that included four children we arrived without much in the way of household goods.

Our apartment at 3921 S. Othello was pretty bare and the kids had very few toys and no yard. So it was probably only natural that Kandi, who was just over a year, made it her past-time to climb up and down the stairs all day long. The problem was she fell down them several times every single day.

We tried a baby gate but that did not work because she was small enough to squeeze through the stair railings. And no matter how many times I took her away from the stairs, sooner or later, while I was preoccupied feeding or changing newborn Kerry, she would be tumbling down them again.

The stairs were wood and she was fair skinned, so she always seemed to have at least one bump on her head or some bruises somewhere. Not only was it traumatic for us to have our toddler constantly getting hurt, but we also feared someone might suspect child abuse.

Finally we came up with a plan. Before we let her out of her crib each morning, we would pray for her safety and protection. We prayed specifically that she would NOT fall down the stairs that day.

The results were amazing! Day after day Kandi climbed on the stairs without incident. Not only that, she had no other accidents anywhere, at any time. We were marking the successful days on our calendar with happy faces and praising the Lord for his protection.

As time went on we weren't so consistent about our daily prayers over Kandi. Yet it only took another fall to remind us. We looked at the calendar and realized it had been 34 days since her last fall. What a lesson in the power of consistent prayer. It is not just something to do because we are told we should. God is actually waiting to hear from us and listening to our petitions. This is perhaps the most amazing thing of all! Just to ponder the fact that the God of the universe took the time to help a little baby down the stairs simply because we asked him to! What is it you need to commit to his care today?

For the Lord thy God
will hold thy right hand,
saying unto thee,
fear not,
I will help thee.
Isaiah 41:13

# STRANGE DOUBLE HEALING

### Seattle, Washington 1973

When I was about seven I fell off of our top bunk. The rail fell ahead of me and I landed on it. I really hurt my back. Though my mom took me to a chiropractor and they gave me some whirlpool treatments it was never the same. It was uncomfortable to sit in the hard chairs at school and it hurt to jump off steps and things, or to lay flat on my back. By the time I was a teenager however, I thought of those problems as normal. I somehow assumed it hurt everyone to hop and jump and sit or lay flat.

Then I further injured my tailbone, when my son Kevin was a toddler. My friend Vicky wanted us to stand on a barrel and make it roll. We lost our balance and I fell on my tailbone and re-injured my back. Still I just put up with it.

My back especially gave me fits during my next three pregnancies. After Kerry was born in September of 1973 I was having problems with pains going down my legs and I was getting tired of it. It amazes me now looking back, that I had not been praying for my back. But I was not grounded in the Word and I guess I had accepted it as "just the way it was" because I had had the problem over half my life.

But during the time Ed was attending Puget Sound College of the Bible, I was at home with our four young children listening to a fiery Evangelist named Shambaugh on the radio who had a healing ministry. After weeks of listening to his daily program it occurred to me that I should ask the Lord to heal my back, which I did.

Instead of feeling instantly better as I had hoped I really didn't feel anything and in fact that day I came down with the flu. The apartment where we were living was not designed with the flu in mind. There was one bathroom in the apartment and it was upstairs. The kitchen, and living room were downstairs, and that is where the kids generally were, so I was forced to run up and down the stairs all day long.

By the time Ed got back from his college classes I was exhausted and still very sick, throwing up and also with diarrhea. He took over with the kids and I went to lie down. Then I had to make another mad dash for the bathroom but I was so lightheaded that when I got there I passed out and fell into the tub hitting my tailbone on the edge of it.

Ed came up and helped me back into bed and started praying for me. "Tonight is that barbeque at the college," he reminded me.

"Ugh!" I replied, even though we had all been looking forward to it since we rarely had any extra money for entertainment. Free events at our church and the college were what we depended on for fun. Ed being the real social one, I knew he was disappointed I did not feel like going.

"Well you take a nap and we'll see how you feel when you wake up. I guess I could always just take the kids."

I nodded, though without much faith. However I did recall a verse I had heard the evangelist quote on the radio, "I tell you the truth, if you have faith as small as a mustard seed, you can say to this mountain, Move from here to there and it will move. Nothing will be impossible for you." Matthew 17:20. Still I did not think I had that much faith.

A few hours later, when I awoke, I lay in bed amazed. I felt refreshed. I felt fine. I was also startled to discover I was laying stretched out flat on my back—a position that I avoided as it had always been painful to me in the past. Yet I felt no pain. I wiggled around and turned this way and that yet the familiar jabs of pain were not there.

"Ed!" I called out joyfully, "Come up here!" When he arrived I had already gotten up and was searching in the closet for what I should wear. "I feel fine. I think I can go to the barbeque.'

"Great!" he said smiling.

"And" I continued, "I think the Lord healed my tailbone by knocking it back in place when I fell in the tub. I didn't realize it then cause I was so sick, but I have no more pain in my back or down my legs!"

So we went to the barbeque and had a great time. I went from throwing up in the afternoon to eating chili dogs and chips that night.

He giveth power to the faint;
and to them that have no
might
he increaseth strength
Isaiah 40:29

# THE SWEETHEARTS BANQUET

### Seattle, Washington 1973

During our Bible college days we were living on next to nothing, yet God always filled our days with good things and good times. We took advantage of every free concert or event going on that we thought that our growing family might enjoy.

There was one event I really wanted to go to but the tickets were just too much. Puget Sound College of the Bible was having a sweetheart's banquet and they had reserved tables in the space needle. I had never been in the space needle and certainly couldn't afford to eat there.

I had even prayed about being able to go somehow and yet as the date drew near no extra provision came in. When the mail came on February 14th I hurried to check it thinking the Lord might send some unexpected money through the mail but nothing was there but advertisements.

I couldn't think of an alternative way the Lord could answer my prayer at this late date so I resigned myself to not going. However—when Ed came home from his afternoon classes he was beaming. He stood there waving two tickets to the sweetheart's banquet.

"How did you manage to pay for those?" I asked, surprised.

"I didn't—they were in my mail box at school. Someone put them there anonymously."

So we hurried and arranged for the neighbor girl, Kim, to baby-sit our four children and scrambled for something appropriate to wear. We had an awesome dinner of filet mignon in the space needle with its awesome view of Seattle.

God makes sure his children find favor and are blessed when they trust in him. Yes, he often uses people to do the blessing, but I am sure it is God that puts the thought into their heart. So anonymous person—we remember your kindness and thank you!

KNOWING THIS,
THAT THE TRYING OF YOUR
FAITH WORKETH PATIENCE.
BUT LET PATIENCE HAVE HER
PERFECT WORK,
THAT YE MAY BE
PERFECT AND ENTIRE,
WANTING NOTHING.
JAMES 1:1-4

# THE SALESMAN

## Seattle, Washington 1974

I was very shy and rarely talked to strangers, so when the pastor of the small Baptist church we were attending began preaching about sharing our faith I began reasoning with the Lord. "You know I can't go out witnessing Lord as I have four small kids to take care of—two in diapers. I am pretty much stuck at home. I would if I could (*which wasn't true*) so if you want me to witness to someone you will have to send them to me."

With that argument I thought I was off the hook and forgot all about it. However the Lord took my words seriously. A short time later a door-to-door salesman knocked on our door.

He began with his sales pitch that I was politely listening too, but then he was apparently distracted by something that was said on the radio. I left my radio on the Christian station 24/7. It kept me encouraged and I figured even when I couldn't hear what was being said over the noise of the kids it would set the atmosphere of our home and at least drive Satan crazy.

So the salesmen stopped his spiel and blurted out, "I wish I knew how to be saved!"

I was so astounded, as I had not even mentioned the Lord, that I think my mouth literally dropped open. "I know how—it's easy—wait here!" And I ran to get one of the Four Steps tracts we had. I probably could have easily led him to the Lord as he was obviously ready, but instead I handed him the tract and said, "Read this, it will tell you how to get saved."

"Thanks," he said, turning to go, already starting to read the track, and forgetting completely what he had knocked on the door for.

*Donna Varnes*

When I closed the door I started laughing. "That was pretty funny Lord—you really got me there—if you send me any more I will try to be better prepared." So the lesson to be learned here is to watch what you say to the Lord. He takes your words seriously and he tests what you say.

Herein is my Father glorified,
that ye bear much fruit,
so shall ye be my disciples.
John 15:8

# THE TERRIBLE COUGH

Seattle, Washington, 1974

When Kandi was about eighteen months old she developed a terrible cough. We took her to the doctor several times over the next couple months. They tried many different medicines and antibiotics but nothing seemed to have any effect on her cough.

Whenever she started coughing she would turn blue and hack and gag till we thought she was going to pass out. They considered the possibility of some kind of allergy and we tried all cotton sheets and no soap and a host of other things but she made no improvement.

Finally after several months they decided she needed to come into the children's hospital for more extensive tests including one for cystic fibrosis and some other dreaded diseases which of course really shook us up. So we scheduled the various tests.

That night we had planned to attend a Christian concert at a local church. Normally we took all four of our children with us wherever we went but we were concerned about taking Kandi out in the night air, so we had the neighbor come stay with her.

This was during the time of the so-called gas shortages, and when we got to the concert it was announced that the group was stranded in another town unable to buy gas, so they had arranged for an evangelist to lead the service instead. He had a healing ministry so naturally his message was about getting healed.

He led us in two great choruses. The lyrics to the first one was "Wonderful, Wonderful, Jesus is to me—Counselor, Prince of Peace, Mighty God is He—Saving me, keeping me, from all sin and shame—Wonderful is my redeemer—praise his name!" The second one that he sang over and over was, "His loving kindness is better than life (2X's) my lips shall praise Him, thus will I bless Him—I will lift up my hands unto His name." He sang them so many times we have never forgotten them.

At the end of the service we went forward to tell him about Kandi and ask him to pray for her. Since she wasn't there he followed the New Testament example of Paul and prayed over a napkin and told us to take it home and place it on her chest.

We hurried home and did so, laying hands on her and praying as he had instructed.

In the morning Kandi woke up and started to cough but we rebuked the cough in Jesus name and claimed her healing, and she never coughed again—not that day or in the days following!

Since she seemed in perfect health now with no symptoms at all, I called and canceled her appointments. A couple days later the doctor called me personally to find out why I had canceled the appointments so of course I explained to him that she had been prayed for and healed. He still urged me to bring her in reminding me how serious her illness could be, and I probably should have, just so they could see for themselves but we never did. Not only was she healed of that cough but I can't remember Kandi becoming seriously ill again till after she grew up and left home.

". . . . I AM THE LORD THAT HEALETH THEE."

EXODUS 15:26

Our family 1974

Kevin, I am holding Kerry
(grannie dresses were in at the time)
Ed is holding Kandi next to Kim

# FEEDING THE ELEVEN

## St Anthony, Idaho 1974

We had just moved to St Anthony, Idaho as our good friends, Dave and Debbie Borup thought Ed could get a job on the Teton Dam. We also wanted to go as God seemed to really be moving in the Spirit filled Baptist church they were attending. Debbie was always telling me of new instances of miraculous healings and prayer answers.

When we first arrived we stayed with them and it was a real eye-opener for me. Debbie prayed about EVERYTHING. One night we had made a chicken dinner for the nine of us but the guys came home from work with two other guests we hadn't planned on.

The men were all laughing about how good everything smelled and how starved they were while we were doing a mental count on how many pieces of chicken we had. I pulled Debbie aside and whispered, "We don't have enough pieces of chicken to go around."

"Yeah I know—let's pray and ask the Lord to multiply it."

*Why not, it happened in the Bible* I thought. So we bowed our heads and prayed. Then we all sat down and said grace and everyone started dishing up. I of little faith however, decided to help God out by just not eating any chicken or much of anything else either. The dishes of food kept being passed around while Debbie kept urging everyone to have some more.

As everyone was finishing up I got up to make me some more tea since I was still hungry. When I came back they were all leaving the table and saying how stuffed they were. I looked at the table in amazement and realized there were lots of leftovers, including two pieces of chicken, a drumstick and thigh, my favorites. "There is still more chicken here," I said.

"I couldn't eat another bite," one of the guys said. Debbie and I smiled as we put up the leftovers and I ate my chicken.

> Jesus fed 5,000 men plus women and children with five loaves of bread and two fish.
> Matthew 14:16-20

# THE EAR INFECTION

### St. Anthony, Idaho 1974

One night I couldn't get one-year-old Kerry to go to sleep. This was a common problem, but tonight he was unusually fussy. Everyone else had gone to sleep except Kerry and I sat down to rock him. It was then I noticed that he kept rubbing his ear so I took a look at it and was shocked to see it was red with pus oozing from it.

We had no money and no insurance only God assurance so I began to pray over him. I did put a heating pad on his ear but mostly we prayed and sang worship songs to the Lord and reminder songs to ourselves. One reminder song for example was: *"God is so good, God is so good, God is so good, He's so good to me, God answers prayer, God answers prayer, God answers prayer, He's so good to me. I love him so, I love him so, I love him so, He's so good to me."*

The more he cried the more I prayed and the more I sang until sometime in the middle of the night we both fell asleep in the rocker. I woke up when Kerry loudly gave the greeting he told me every morning—"I'm hungry!"

I tried to look in his ear but he squirmed away and ran for the refrigerator, repeating his mantra "I'm hungry!"

Finally as he sat in his high chair eating oatmeal I was able to look in his ear. It was no longer red and it was no longer draining pus. "Does your ear hurt?" I asked, but he just kept eating.

When he was done he started yanking at the door—he wanted out in the yard to play. "Wait for your brother and sisters," I said, "and you have to get dressed first." He tore upstairs to get them out of bed.

Later that day I was sharing with the neighbor lady about how Kerry was healed from his ear infection. She attended church, though a different denomination, so I was surprised when she said, "You can't just pray away an ear infection! He needs antibiotics or it will just get worse."

I pointed to Kerry who was running around the yard happily playing, and said, "Well look at him—he's definitely been healed!"

It didn't matter how much he APPEARED to be healed—she still ended our conversation abruptly by stating, "Well I have to go but you need to get him into the doctor right away!"

Not only did she make me feel I was being neglectful, but looking back, considering other conversations, I think it also ruffled her feathers just to think that God would answer our prayers at all, for we didn't attend THEIR church. My reality clashed with her theology.

And concerning Kerry—I can't remember his ever having another ear infection or ear problem growing up. When God heals—he heals!

He cast out the spirits with his word
And healed all that were sick

Mathew 8:16

# THE HEADACHE PRAYER

### St Anthony, Idaho 1975

One afternoon we were traveling in our old yellow station wagon with our four kids. Kerry, who was two at the time, complained his head hurt. I started rummaging through my purse and the glove box looking for some baby aspirin or something that might help. Finding nothing, I said "Well we will just have to pray and ask the Lord to make your headache go away." (Why I hadn't done that first I don't know.) I said a simple prayer over him and he flipped back over the seat into the back. (This was before seat belt laws and car seats)

He began goofing off in the back seat with his brother and sisters as he usually did, but was getting more rambunctious than usual so I hollered back, "You better settle down! That's not going to help your headache!"

I'll never forget the surprised and confused look on his face as he declared, "It doesn't hurt—we prayed—remember?"

THE POWER OF THE LORD WAS

PRESENT TO HEAL THEM.

LUKE 5:17

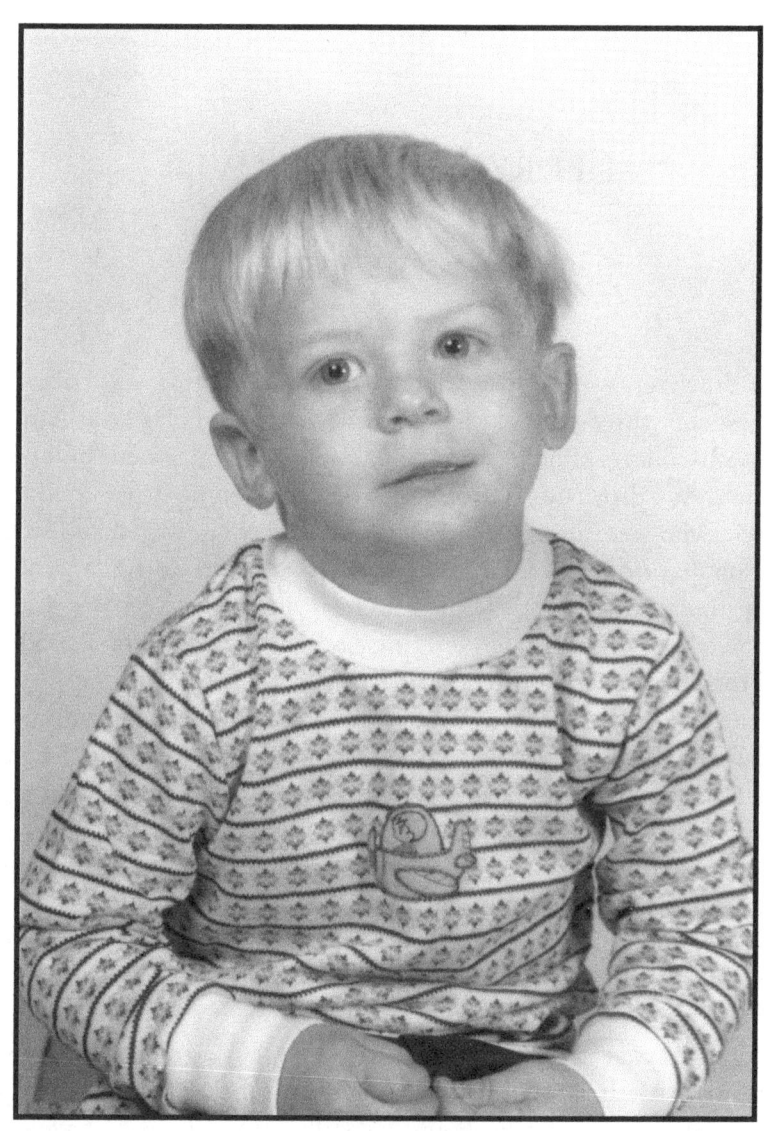

Kerry Varnes, age three

# KERRY GETS RAN OVER

## Tulsa, Oklahoma 1976

Robin Smeltzer, was a close friend who lived near us and babysat my youngest son, three-year-old Kerry while I attended classes at American Christian College. One Saturday our four kids and I were invited over for lunch. As I drove our station wagon up the sloping driveway their five children, who were already out in their yard playing, waved and smiled.

After parking, my kids, Kevin, Kim, Kandi, and Kerry, started joining theirs in the yard, while I went inside to help Robin get lunch ready. We were chatting while fixing up plates when all of a sudden we heard the children screaming outside.

I ran out the door just in time to see our station wagon rolling down the driveway. Then horrified I saw Kerry, was holding up his hands against the open car door as if he fully expected to stop the heavy car with his little body.

Before I could get to him the open car door knocked him down and the car ran over him and kept going down the driveway. In a daze I ran to where he lay on the ground. I gathered him up praying silently while Robin began firing orders. "You kids get in the car—we're going to the hospital."

Kerry started screaming and crying in my arms, and thrashing around which was actually a welcome sound, but I tried to calm him, remembering that he really should lay still. I think I would have just sat there in my state of shock if Robin hadn't been there with the presence of mind to act quickly.

As Robin sped towards the hospital, and I sat holding Kerry, the kids explained how they had all gotten into the car, pretending to go on a trip.

When it got knocked out of gear and started rolling down the driveway they all jumped out, but Kerry tried to stop the car.

Then Robin noticed that the gas gauge was on empty and realized we didn't have enough gas to get to the hospital. It seemed bizarre to be stopping for gas in such an emergency—something that never happened in the movies.

After dropping Kerry and I off at the emergency room, Robin went and got Ed who was attending Spartan School of Aeronautics. He soon joined me in my nerve wracking wait while the ER doctors examined Kerry.

While we were in the waiting room another family came in whose son was also run over but by a much smaller car, and he was in intensive care, in a coma, not expected to make it. This of course increased our fears over Kerry.

Kerry however was not in a coma. We could hear him crying even out in the waiting room. This of course was still very distressing as I imagined what intense pain he must be in. Finally, when they let us back in after his initial x-rays and tests, I kissed him and asked, "Kerry where do you hurt the most?"

"I'm hungry!" he wailed. "I want my lunch!"

Startled but amused, I realized they never got to eat their dished up plates of food. "I'll go ask the doctor if you can have something to eat."

"No. He can't have anything to eat or drink." The doctor said, "He probably has internal injuries. I'm going in to look over the test results right now. But we are going to start him on an IV. That should help him to not feel as hungry."

I went back to Kerry with a sense of dread. Not only did I have to tell him he couldn't eat, but how could I prepare him for the additional trauma of them sticking a needle in his arm. He hated immunization shots and it was always a tearful fight to give them to him.

"Kerry," I started out quietly, "You can't put any food in your tummy right now, it may be hurt, but they are going to bring in an IV and poke a little hole in your arm and feed you that way."

Amazingly, Kerry immediately stopped crying. "Okay," he said calmly. About that time the nurse came in wheeling the IV machine.

"See, your food is in this bag," I explained.

He looked at it curiously and waited expectantly. The nurse took his arm and poked the needle into it. Kerry sat perfectly still without making a sound, watching her set everything up. Then the nurse left and Kerry lay staring at his arm for several minutes. Suddenly he burst into tears and wailed loudly, "I'm still hungry!"

When the Doctor came in next he was the one amazed. The only real injury was a cracked pelvic bone. He could eat! They wanted to keep him a day or two for observation but then he could probably heal up fine at home. The main thing was he needed to lie still and rest.

We were so relieved and thankful to the Lord—but how could we get Kerry to lie still? We went out and bought him a coloring book and crayons and several books, but he just pretended the crayons were airplanes and sent them soaring across the room, and tried to build structures with his books.

Finally on the day he got to come home the doctor instructed us, "Now I want him to stay in bed and not walk for 30 days."

"How are we going to make him do that?" I asked.

"Oh, he won't want to do much moving around—the pain should keep him still," he replied.

But at home we had problems keeping Kerry down from the start. We awoke the very next morning to discover he was in bed with us. He had apparently walked from his bedroom to ours.

Still I tried hard to keep him lying still. He wanted to be wherever I was so I laid him on a big pillow and moved him from room to room with me all day long. I had to remind him constantly to lie back down. All my attempts were useless. Within a few days nothing slowed him down.

We were instructed to bring him back for a check-up after that first month. The instant we pulled into the parking lot of the hospital, Kerry got hysterical. He screamed non-stop all the way to the doctor's office. Luckily they got him right in. I was asked to undress him. Kerry began kicking and thrashing around to keep me from undressing him. He did not want the doctor to look at him.

Finally the doctor stopped me and said, "If he can put up a fight like that about getting undressed, he must be doing pretty well." And so we left without the exam. We are certain it was God who protected his life as well as speedily healed his body.

". . . . AND WITH HIS STRIPES

WE ARE HEALED."

ISAIAH 53:5

# THE FROG PRAYER

## Tulsa, Oklahoma 1976

We tried to teach our children about faith and prayer, but looking back I realize they had plenty of faith to begin with.

We lived in Tulsa, Oklahoma the year Kandi attended Kindergarten. Ed and I thought it was important for the kids, Kevin, Kim, Kandi, and Kerry, to learn to pray for anything that was of a concern to them personally. God seemed to take special care to answer their little prayers. The frog prayer, however, never even got asked.

The kids were gathered around Ed and I and we asked each in turn what their prayer requests were, and then all of us prayed together about it.

"What do you want to pray for Kandi?" Ed asked.

"My frog" she answered solemnly.

"What's the matter with your frog? Ed asked.

She ran to the window and brought back a jar and handed it to Ed. "I wanted him to be able to see out the window, but I forgot about him," she said sorrowfully. She looked at the floor, the whole weight of her world on her shoulders.

Ed took the jar, so he could get a good look. He tried hard to stifle a smile and maintain the serious atmosphere in which Kandi had shared her request. But he couldn't do it. He quickly shoved the jar into my hands and hurried out of the room.

Puzzled, I peered into the jar. I expected to see a sickly frog. Kandi's pet resembled a frog in shape only. The hot Tulsa sun, piercing through the window, had sucked it drier than any dehydrator could have. The frog lay flat and parched at the bottom of the jar like an ancient scrap of paper.

I am not arguing with anyone as to whether God "could" have revived that frog. But any sliver of faith I possessed fled as I shook the jar a bit and saw the frog start to crumble. I couldn't even bring myself to ask. I realized that Kandi already had more faith than I did.

"I think we should bury it Honey." I said, with as much seriousness as I could muster.

So we had a funeral for that frog. Afterwards, Kevin, "the expert," told Kandi, "See, I told you it wasn't good to lie out in the sun."

"... According to your faith
be it unto you."

Matthew 9:29

# IS THIS REGULAR FOOD OR DO WE HAVE TO PRAY OVER IT?

### Tulsa, Oklahoma 1977

After we moved to the house on the Oxley farm, Ed began framing houses with Chuck Smeltzer. He then convinced his brother-in-law, Al Beach, to move to Tulsa so the three of them could start their own framing business which they named ACE Framing Contractors, using the first letter of each of their names.

Since we only had a small two bedroom house, we had to set up a roll-away bed in the kitchen every night for Al to sleep on and he had to get it up and out of the way each morning before I could fix breakfast.

Now that I was cooking for seven I really had to stretch the food dollar. I asked the Lord to help me in that department by always praying my store prayer, "Lord let everything I need be on sale." Which he always seemed to honor—to such a degree that I began thinking that if there was something I wanted and it was NOT on sale—then the Lord must not want me to buy it. I also frequently asked the Lord to help me in creating meals out of what I had as I never wanted to throw any leftovers out, and of course we always blessed the food we ate as well as praying it would be enough to fill every one up.

Al however thought I sometimes got a little carried away—especially after the picnic incident. It gets very hot in Tulsa in the summer and we did not have air-conditioning, so we often went to Keystone Lake to swim and cool off. Of course we always took a picnic basket with us, and this time, because it was Sunday, the day of the week I splurged on meat or poultry as the main dish, I had packed fried chicken, and potato salad.

When we got home I asked everyone to bring in the food and stuff from the car, and optimistically thought that they had. It was so hot that night that Ed and I lay a blanket out on the grass and slept outside.

After another hot day I opened the refrigerator, contemplating dinner and looking for the leftovers from the picnic. The watermelon was there and the ice tea but not the chicken or the potato salad. I ran out to the car and was horrified to see them still sitting out in the hot sun. I rushed them into the house praying as I went, for what were we going to have for dinner if the leftovers had gone bad? After blessing the food I smelled the chicken and the potato salad. They smelled alright so I took a little taste of each. They tasted alright. So I put the potato salad in the fridge and the chicken in the oven. Later as we sat down to eat I said, "Oh, don't forget to bless the food!" I guess there must have been something in my tone of voice as Al looked at me and the food suspiciously but dished up anyway. I never said a word.

As they were eating Ed said, "This potato salad tastes even better than yesterday!" I just smiled.

The next night at dinner I felt safe in telling about the remarkable thing the Lord had done with the food left out in the car. Al was shocked I had served it, and from then on, when we sat down to eat he would ask, "Is this regular food, or do we have to pray over it?"

"... AND IF THEY DRINK ANY

DEADLY THING,

IT SHALL NOT HURT THEM; ..."

MARK 16:18

# THE MISSING FINGER

### Tulsa, Oklahoma 1977

We were renting a little house at 4007 North Memorial Avenue where our four children had plenty of room to run and play. One day ten-year-old Kevin, had asked me permission to do something and I told him no.

He got angry and went back outside slamming the door as he left. Immediately I heard him scream in pain and I ran to see what the matter was. He had slammed his middle finger in the door and blood was spurting out all over.

I hate the sight of blood and so I immediately covered it with a clean wash rag which was quickly soaked in blood. Alarmed I told everyone to jump in the car we were taking him to the hospital.

The doctor in ER removed the soaked rag and took a look at the still bleeding finger and asked, "Did you bring the rest of his finger?"

I looked at him dumbfounded and shook my head no.

"Your son has cut off the tip of his finger just below the fingernail."

I made myself look and sure enough his finger was now shorter than the fingers on each side.

"If you had brought it with you I could have reattached it. But if too much time has passed it won't work. It is too late to go back for it. I'll just have to clean it up and fold the skin over the end, and stitch it. He won't ever have a fingernail since he has cut it off well below the nail bed, but his finger should heal up fine if you keep it clean. I'll also give him some antibiotics to ward off an infection."

Soon Kevin was stitched and bandaged. We picked up his prescription and went home. Kevin ran to the door and looked. Sure enough, the tip of his finger was stuck on the doorjamb. His complete fingernail was there. The finger was grey and morbid looking so I told him to go throw it in the trash.

The next day however, I learned he had taken it to school for show-and-tell, and grossed-out his teacher and most of the students. However, perhaps they learned a lesson on why you should not lose your temper and slam doors.

But this is not the end of the story. We always had prayer time with the children before they went to bed so of course I suggested we pray for Kevin's finger—that it would heal up quickly with no infection. Kevin however added, "And please Lord—help my finger nail to grow back."

I quickly reminded him what the doctor had told us and ended with, "So there is no use praying your fingernail will grow back. We should just pray it heals quickly."

Regardless, every night Kevin's prayer was, "And please Lord—help my fingernail grow back." Finally I gave up and let him pray whatever way he wanted. Miraculously—in a couple of months, Kevin's fingernail grew back and his finger was getting longer again!

Today, if you were to look at Kevin's hand, you would notice that his middle finger is only slightly shorter than it should be, but it has a full fingernail. I think the Lord left it just slightly different to remind him and us of the miracle we had witnessed. Whenever I look at that fingernail I am reminded of God's promise in Mathew 9: 29, "According to your faith be it unto you.

It shall be done for you

as you have believed

Mathew 8:13

# ACCIDENTS, TORNADOS AND THE RED SPORTS CAR

## Tulsa, Oklahoma 1977

I have never liked to drive so if there is ANYONE who wants to—I let them. So it was one day when my friend Robin and I had some errands to run that I asked her to drive our station wagon.

We were turning left onto a boulevard which had high unmowed grass. A little, low riding, red sports car was coming towards us but we were unable to see it. Robin clipped the front end causing some damage mainly to the other car.

I hated to have Robin pay for the damages, after all, I had asked her to drive, and it really seemed the city should have kept the grass cut on the boulevard to increase visibility. Both our families were barely scraping by and this was yet another unexpected expense. So we prayed.

The next few weeks the other driver got their estimates on fixing the damage and when the letter arrived we just shook our heads wondering how either of us could pay it. Again we prayed asking for God's help. Then a strange blessing happened.

Tulsa had a big storm with tornados and flooding. It seems the red sports car was totaled. Her insurance paid for the car so we were informed that since one claim on the car had already paid for the damages, she could not be paid twice for the same car and all expenses to us were dropped.

God has a way of taking care of His own, often in ways we could never come up with and sometimes even when we are at fault. He offers us His grace and unmerited favor.

All things work together

for good to them

that love God . . .

Romans 8:28

# THE SONG GOD GAVE AND TOOK AWAY

### Tulsa, Oklahoma 1978

Ed always had a gift for music and whenever we drove somewhere in the car we sang songs to the Lord. Often times the Lord would inspire Ed by giving him a new chorus.

Though I was writing stories, poems and essays even back then, the Lord had never given me a song, and one day after Ed shared yet another beautiful chorus the Lord had given him, I asked the Lord about it. "I want you to give ME a song too Lord."

The very next time I was driving home from my classes at American Christian College, the Lord put a song on my heart. I happily sang it all the way home.

Whenever I found myself alone I sang the song the Lord gave to me. Eventually the newness of the song wore off and I hadn't been singing it for a while. Then I tried to remember it but couldn't. After struggling to recall the tune for several minutes I said, "Lord—help me remember my song."

Immediately he spoke to my heart, "Why? You weren't sharing it with anyone." I never did remember how the song went.

If that were to happen to me today I hope I have grown in the Lord enough to keep my promise to Him that I would indeed share his song with everyone who'd listen. However, at that time, the thought of singing the song for anyone—even family, unnerved me, so I didn't want to make any rash promises. I let Ed get the songs from then on without complaint.

There is a Bible principle found in the parable of the talents in Mathew 25. It tells the story of the master giving talents to his servants. Two of them used their talents well to bring increase and one was afraid and hid what he was given. In the parable the Lord of the house returned, praised the ones who had used their talent and gave them more to work with, but the one who was afraid, and did not use his talent, the Lord took the little he had and gave it to the one who had done the best with what the Lord had given him.

So if you find me tracking you down to share what the Lord has given me, be it a story, a song, or an insight, you will understand why. I want to be in the group that used what they were given, no matter how little or much, to the fullest extent.

Take therefore the talent
from him,
and give it unto him
which hath ten talents.
Matthew 25:28

Our Family in 1978

Donna, Kerry, Kim, Kandi, Kevin and Ed

# THE LITTLE HOTDOG PRAYER

## Tulsa, Oklahoma 1978

My husband Ed and I made the perfect prayer team. He had faith to believe God for the really big things like a terminal illness or moving to a new town with just enough money to get there. I had faith to pray for all the little day to day things like the items we needed would be on sale or asking the Lord for a good parking spot. So between the two us of we had everything covered: the big and the little things.

It was a typical hot day in Tulsa so after church one Sunday, I invited my friend Kay to go with us to Keystone Lake. It was the most economical thing to do with a family of six. We packed a big picnic lunch plus towels, blankets, inner tubes and sunscreen. I set it all by the door—ready to go.

As I was heading out to the car with the potato salad I hollered, "Everyone grab the stuff by the door—it's time to go." The problem is I never checked to see who grabbed what. The thought never occurred to me till we were about half way there.

"Did you get the bag of charcoal by the door?" I asked Ed.

"No, I didn't see it."

Now the picnic area around Keystone was not like Montana, where we came from. You couldn't just scrounge around the woods to find stuff to make a fire from, you had to bring it with you. "Well I guess we'll have to pray there is still some charcoal in the grill. Wait—I think I forgot to get the starter fluid—did you get it?—and I don't have any matches—do you?"

"No," he said.

"Well I guess we'll have to pray that the coals in the grill are still hot."

"Why don't you just pray for the hot dogs to be there too?" asked Ed sarcastically.

"I didn't forget the hotdogs. But if I needed the hot dogs, don't you think he could provide those too?"

"Yes." Ed said. "But why should he bother when we should have checked?"

"If God could make the heavens and earth in seven days, how much trouble do you think it would be for him to make hot dogs—poof—there they'd be—no effort at all. But we don't need the hot dogs, just hot coals in the grill," I said.

When we finally pulled into Keystone Lake picnic area I began looking for a likely campsite with hot coals. "Look—there is a family just leaving—let's try there!" So as they drove off, we pulled in and I jumped out of our station wagon and ran to check their grill.

When I got there I began to laugh. "Ed you have got to see this—come here!" I giggled.

Ed, Kay, and all the kids gathered round and stared in awe. The grill not only contained hot coals but sitting on top was seven perfectly cooked hot dogs—one for each of us!

God is not only able—he is willing!

He gave them bread from heaven to eat.

John 6:31

# STRETCHING THE LAST GALLON

## Montana to Tulsa, Oklahoma trip 1978

We had been living in Tulsa Oklahoma for almost two years and greatly missed our families in Montana and Wyoming. Ed had been doing some creative accounting on our checkbook ledger. When he deducted a purchase he always rounded up to the next dollar amount, so if the check was for $14.39, he subtracted $15. The day came when he calculated we had enough money to make a trip back home, so we packed up our bags and four children, Kevin, Kim, Kandi and Kerry and headed to Montana. Round trip it was about 3500 miles.

We were having a great time visiting with various relatives and friends but the time came when we had to head back to Tulsa. We were saying our goodbyes at Ed's cousin's house, Derrel Lee. They had a 16 year old son that had been having a hard time with life and Derrel got the idea in his head that it would do him a world of good to have a change of scenery and go with us. We were willing so he called him in.

"Hey Jeff, do you want to go with Ed and Donna to Oklahoma for a while?"

"When?"

"We were just getting ready to leave. How quick could you grab your things?" Ed laughed. Jeff seemed uncertain but with the three of us egging him on he decided to go and within the hour we were out the door.

It wasn't till we were hours away that Jeff discovered we didn't actually have enough money to get back to Tulsa. We had spent more on our trip than we had figured. We needed seven tanks of gas and we had enough for about three. Of course we had already told the Lord about the problem and we were anticipating his help.

Jeff however was nervous. You could almost tell by the look on his face that he was thinking, "How did I get stuck with these crazy relatives who keep singing: *Give me gas in my Ford, keep me trucking for the Lord, give me gas in my Ford I pray—Hallelujah!*—and every other Jesus chorus they knew?"

We had seen the Lord come through for us time and time again, often through people, so we were thinking perhaps one of our friends or relatives or a complete stranger on our return trip would give us some money. However, when God sees that we are depending on people too much, or that we are expecting him to answer our prayers in a certain way, he delights in doing something new and unexpected.

When we left the home of the last person we knew on our route and we had only enough for one more tank of gas, we knew it was one of those times. Jeff was even more nervous now. "What are you going to do?"

"Keep going," Ed said. When we filled the tank with the last of our money and headed East, Jeff kept his eyes glued on the gas gauge. It was going down just as it always did.

I reminded him, "God only has to stretch the last gallon." But he kept staring at the gauge in a worried fashion and not joining in with our singing at all. Finally Ed placed his empty wallet in front of the gas gauge so he couldn't see it.

We were long overdue for a fill-up and so we knew God was indeed stretching our gas. Each extra mile we went we rejoiced. We couldn't stop and buy food either but different family and friends had sent us away with homemade bread and jelly, apples off their tree and a real prize—a gallon of honey from Ed's sister, Mary, who had her own bee hives. "John the Baptist lived on locusts and honey," I said. "I think I will stick to just the honey," and I put a spoonful in my mouth.

We were in Wichita, Kansas, just 175 miles from home, when we ran out of gas. We were a little confused. After all God had undeniably stretched our last tank of gas. Even Jeff couldn't dispute that. So why didn't he stretch it all the way home?"

Ed coasted into a gas station. "What are we going to do now?" Jeff asked, "Call the police?" His dad was a police officer so that was the first thing that came to mind.

Ed however went inside to borrow a phone and called a local pastor. He came down and filled our tank and we wrote him a check to hold for we knew we had a paycheck coming that Friday. This pastor however, also invited the seven of us over for dinner at his house. This greatly surprised Jeff who couldn't believe that someone would do all this for complete strangers. We had a great time of fellowship and then went on our way.

The funny thing is that our gas mileage went back to normal and it took about the same amount of money to get those last 175 miles as it had the previous 350. I think the Lord wanted to show Jeff the love of God through that generous pastor whom God had prepared to bless us.

And my God will meet all your needs according to his glorious riches in Christ Jesus.
Philippians 4:19

# HE SET ME IN A LARGE PLACE

## Gillette, Wyoming 1980-1986

Some prayers take years before they are answered, and this was one of them. We had moved to Gillette, Wyoming and were living in the basement of my Mother's house with our six children when I sighed to the Lord that I would love to have our own place—a big place—with room for the kids to run around and not bother anyone.

Later a verse jumped out at me in the Bible: Psalm 118:4-6, "Let them now that fear the LORD say, that his mercy endureth forever. I called upon the LORD in my distress: the LORD answered me, and set me in a large place."

I felt certain the Lord was speaking directly to me. I was confident he had heard me and intended to set us in some large place. Months later when we were able to rent a townhouse I considered whether this was the place the Lord spoke of, but it was side-by-side other townhouses and I had pictured a place I really didn't have to worry about the noise and the next door neighbors. Even the next year when we bought a house with a basement, it was still in a subdivision.

It wasn't until after we moved to Alaska in 1984, and my husband, my oldest son and I were each drawn for 20 acre homestead parcels, that the promise was truly fulfilled. Alaska is the largest state, virtually empty with only two people per square mile. And there we were given a piece of property big enough so that the kids could go outside and holler to their hearts content.

I had almost given up and totally wrote off the promise of that verse after the first couple of years of waiting. But, one day when we were all standing on the ridge of our property, over-looking the Nenana River Valley, the Lord brought the verse to mind again: "the LORD answered me, and set me in a large place." I looked around in awe and thought, *he certainly did*!

If you have a promise from the Lord, keep believing and patiently waiting for it to come to pass. Don't be like Abraham and Sarah who had received a promise from God, but decided to settle for something less than what they had hoped. I too almost settled for less, thinking perhaps he had meant something different than the true desire of my heart. What I have discovered is God more often goes way beyond our expectations if we don't lose heart or faith.

I was dreaming of a home in the country with a big yard and room between neighbors, he gave our family 60 acres near Denali National Park!

Now unto him that is able to do exceeding abundantly above all that we ask or think, according to the power that worketh in us,
Ephesians 3:20

# OUR DAILY BREAD ISN'T PRACTICAL LORD

### Heron, Montana 1981

There were many other prayer answers that occurred while the one about the large place was on hold. We kept trying to make it happen. Reflecting back, our time in Heron better prepared us for our homesteading experience in Alaska still four years in the future.

We sold our house in Gillette, Wyoming in 1980 and moved with our good friends Robin and Chuck Smeltzer and their two kids, to a parcel of property that butted up against state forest land in Heron, Montana. We wanted to raise our five children in a wholesome farm setting and work for ourselves living more of a subsistence lifestyle.

We had several ideas for making some income. We were raising rabbits. In fact we had over 500 and we had invested some money in a load of antiques to resell in California. From the sale of our house and the antiques we were able to get set up with a monarch wood stove and a pick up load of farm animals: a goat, some wiener pigs, some chickens and a couple ducks. And we started home-schooling our kids.

We had also filled barrels with flour and sugar and other staples, when we had moved in. Chuck Smeltzer knew how to get that Monarch wood stove at just the right temperature so his wife Robin could bake homemade bread. It was always excellent!

It was a wonderful experience that I wouldn't have wanted to miss but we weren't really cut out to be farmers. For one thing none of us liked to butcher anything. I loved raising all the baby animals, watching the chicks run around—but we put off having them for dinner as a last resort. And the vegetables I put up for the winter from our garden ran out about the end of December.

Because of some trucker strike, the Canadian company stopped coming down to buy our rabbits. Then some sort of illness swept through those remaining, and things got a little tough.

We always seemed to have enough food for the 11 of us to make it through the day, but were always wondering about tomorrow. God came through again and again for our group—an odd job here or the sale of something there. Each time we got a little money we would drive the ten miles into Clark Fork, Idaho to buy much needed supplies.

What bugged me was I never seemed to have enough to buy in bulk where the real savings would be. I always seemed to have just enough to meet our immediate needs. Plus the constant trips to town with our gas guzzling pick-up were just another expense.

One day I began reasoning with the Lord. "Lord I know you have been supplying our daily bread—but Lord, it is just not practical to run into town every day or two to get what we need for dinner. We need to get things in bulk—to stock up and have our pantry filled." Looking back I remembered how many times I had simply prayed, "Lord, what are we going to have for dinner?" Perhaps he had been waiting for me to say just this sort of—thinking ahead—prayer.

It seemed so anyway, for in just a few days we got some visitors. A couple had sold their restaurant and they had a bunch of these gallon sized cans of food they didn't know what to do with. It was just too big of a size for the two of them. They had heard we had a household with seven kids and wondered if we could use them.

Could we!!! We gratefully helped them unload all the cans which filled our little pantry to the top. God and God's people are so awesome!

Whoever has will be
given more,
and he will have an
abundance.
Matthew 13:12

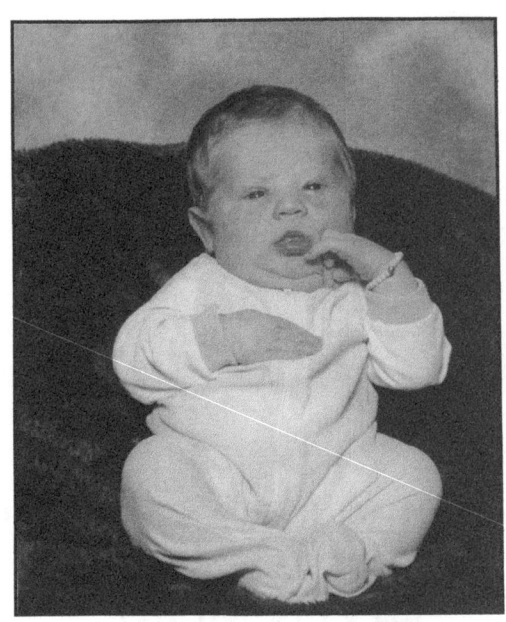

Baby Kody six days old 1982

Kody and Katrina 1983

# THE DIAPER PRAYER

Gillette, Wyoming 1982

When our sixth child, Kody, was born in 1982, I was still hanging on to the 1950's attitude that disposable diapers were an extravagant luxury, and that "good" mothers would chose to wash out cotton diapers rather than subject their baby to wearing those paper and plastic things. It was actually the Lord that caused me to discard that opinion.

We were back living in a basement apartment in Gillette on Ptarmigan Avenue, and did not have our own washer and dryer. I only had a dozen cloth diapers, so I was constantly scrambling to keep up a clean supply.

When I went to the store I often walked through the baby aisle and invariably stopped yet again to compare the cost and other pros and cons of the cloth diapers versus the disposable ones. But I didn't really have the extra funds to buy either.

One day after I just finished rinsing a dirty diaper out in the toilet and putting it in the almost full diaper pail to be laundered I sighed. "Lord I either need a lot more cloth diapers or a bunch of those disposable ones. The disposable ones would be nice, but they are pretty expensive, so I'll leave the choice to you."

Shortly after that conversation with the Lord we came home from church to discover someone had anonymously left a box of groceries and a case of disposable diapers sitting in front of our door. I almost cried with joy for it not only spoke of someone's thoughtfulness and willingness to be led by the Lord, but it spoke volumes about the character of God.

God is not miserly or stingy. He is a loving and extravagant God who cares about our everyday lives and concerns. Even more faithfully than any of our human relationships, when we love and trust God he responds back. He constantly demonstrates how well he knows us and loves us and how closely he is paying attention to our every word, thought and action. God provides for his children. What a loving Father.

I WILL BLESS HER WITH
ABUNDANT PROVISIONS:
HER POOR WILL I SATISFY WITH
FOOD.
PSALMS 132:14

# THE PRIME RIB STORY

### Gillette, Wyoming 1983

We were living in Gurley Trailer Court, and despite Ed working as a mail carrier for the school district and me cleaning houses several times a week, money was tight. Every payday I bought a case of macaroni and cheese and a case of Ramen noodles because it was so cheap. Luckily, our six children were happy to eat either one for dinner by itself if we ran out of meat or vegetables and those leftovers could be added to either so nothing went to waste.

One day after a particularly long stretch of our mostly pasta dinners I sighed to the Lord, "Lord I know you only promised to provide our daily bread, and nobody else in the house seems to mind, but I sure am tired of eating Ramen and macaroni and cheese. I realize we are not going to starve or anything but I sure would like a really good meal for a change—like some meat!" (Now didn't I sound like the children of Israel wandering in the desert?)

However, God did not seem to mind my asking. That night when Ed got home from work he had a big smile on his face. "Go get in the car I have a surprise."

As we drove towards town I thought, *maybe the Lord blessed us with some unexpected money.*

Then Ed looked over at the gas gauge and said, "I sure hope we don't run out of gas." So I knew he didn't get any money.

He drove into the Prime Rib restaurant, one of the most expensive places in town. I was dumbfounded. "I won a prime rib dinner for two today!" he said beaming. It was some call in radio contest.

So we had a delightful dinner with real meat as the main course just as I had asked for. God is so good and so generous. I would have been pleased to have had a pound of hamburger to cook, but he went all out.

The blessings continued. Ed kept winning that contest over and over again. The prizes were always different. We won a food dehydrator, some pewter goblets and so many other prizes that some of the workers at Ed's job were mad at him even though there was no way he could control whose name they drew. They were so jealous I think the Lord decided he better find a new way to bless us.

... put me to the test,
says the Lord of hosts,
see if I will not open the
windows of heaven for you
and pour down for you a
blessing until there is no
more need.

Malachi 3:10

# THE MILK PRAYER

### 1985 Wasilla, Alaska

We had moved to Alaska with our friends the Smeltzers, July of 1984, and believe me it was difficult to find housing for four adults, eight children, two dogs and a cat. We finally found a place to rent out on Hollywood and Vine, though the gravel roads and surrounding woods seemed the exact opposite of that location in LA.

I had attended a presentation about Montessori educational methods while living in Gillette and so when I read in the Anchorage Daily News about Tom Thumb Montessori School, (preschool through sixth) I was excited. I wanted our four youngest to attend there despite the fact it was 50 miles away and we couldn't really afford it.

I also enrolled in their one year teacher certification program which involved a half day of lecture and the other half actually co-teaching with a seasoned Montessori teacher. Starting with day one, I was putting into practice what I was learning, and I loved it. Regardless, of the hardships, this was an awesome opportunity. However, it meant that much of our resources were going to pay for tuition and travel expenses. Sometimes we didn't get home till bedtime. Chuck and Ed were also working out of town, so that left Robin Smeltzer at home stuck with most of the cooking.

Since she did the cooking—when she asked if a university student from their church who needed housing, could stay with us too, we agreed. Howard Merken came from a well-to-do east coast family with only two brothers and no pets, and so he spent much of his time at our house, in a state of shock.

For a joke, I put a scripture verse above the stove for Robin that read "FEED MY SHEEP"—which she did good-naturedly. She seemed to be able to make awesome meals out of little to nothing which is what she had to work with most of the time.

You can imagine how fast a group of 13 could go through the milk, and I often heard Robin say at night, "stay out of the milk, we need it for breakfast in the morning.

Though I knew she was right, I had grown up without any limits placed on what I ate or drank and it bugged me that we should have to limit our children. After all, milk was good for them. So I took it up with the Lord. "Lord, I want my children to be able to drink as much milk as they want. I don't want to have to ration it." Of course I was thinking of one of us getting a raise or something so we could afford to buy more milk, but God is more creative than that. In fact I think he gets a kick out of letting us come up with our best solution and then doing something completely different than anything we could think up. That is exactly what he did this time.

A few days after my milk prayer, a man called Ed on the phone and asked if we could use some milk. Ed of course said yes. He told Ed he had a lot of it, and Ed assured him we could share it with anyone who needed it and would announce it at our church as well. But when the man arrived we were stunned.

He had the back of his pick-up heaped with gallons, quarts and pints of milk. Since it was winter in Alaska they were all frozen so we just unloaded them into the shed and unthawed them as we needed them. There was Whole milk, skim milk, half and half, chocolate milk, strawberry milk, buttermilk and every other conceivable kind of milk.

I began to laugh. It was as if God was saying, "You didn't say which kind of milk you wanted, so I sent them all."

This man brought us loads of milk like this several times that year and we never had to limit the kids on their milk drinking again. He also brought us big bags of donuts and bread. Our kids were always on the skinny side so we didn't have to limit them on that either. It is good to remember that we serve a God who has no limits.

Therefore I tell you,
do not be anxious about
your life,
what you will eat or
what you will drink...
Matthew 6:25

# THE BLUE STATION WAGON

### Wasilla, Alaska 1985

We had driven up the Alcan Highway with our 1976, 15 passenger van and had put lots of miles on it. Finally though, after being in Alaska a while the engine went out and we were without a vehicle. Our friends, the Smeltzer's, were living with us at the time making twelve of us, and they only had a pick-up.

So when the kids came home from school I got out a paper and pen and wrote 'Lord we need a new vehicle' across the top. Then I said "let's pray for another vehicle." I like to get kids involved in praying whenever I can as they seem to have a lot less trouble with doubt and unbelief compared to adults.

My friend Robin sat down at the table with me and said, "Well it needs to be at least a seven passenger vehicle." I wrote that down.

After having numerous vehicles that required you to have special training in how to get them to start and run, I quipped, "I want to be able to start it by just turning on the key. AND I want a really good heater." The kids agreed. The big van had seemed impossible to keep warm during our Alaskan winters.

Then fourteen-year-old Kim got involved. "I don't want it to be green." That was Ed's favorite color and the color of our old van as well as lots of other things Ed picked out. It was definitely NOT Kim's favorite color.

Ed, Chuck and Kevin were not home at the time so we didn't get their input. We held hands and prayed and folded the paper and stuck it in our Bible.

We were attending Missions North Church at the time, as were Rocky and Evenette Greenfield. Rocky called Ed from the car dealership in Anchorage where he worked and said, "I heard your van broke down. I have a station wagon you can have if you want to come pick it up."

The kids and I were all excited when we heard the news. We couldn't wait to see it. When Ed got back with it we all ran outside. It was blue!—so Kim was pleased. It had jump seats in the back-end so we could seat more than seven—so Robin was happy. I sat in the driver's seat and turned the key without even pumping the gas and it immediately started up. I flipped the switch for the heater and it blasted me with hot air—I had to turn it down. The kids and I were enthusiastically sharing our prayer list with Ed, Kevin and Chuck who hadn't seen it before.

Everyone was happy but seventeen-year-old Kevin. "Well I wish you would have asked what I wanted," he said. "I would have added that it should look cool."

"Well a little red sports car would not be that practical for our bunch," I said, and we all laughed.

Delight thyself also
in the LORD;
and he shall give thee the
desires of thine heart.

Psalms 37:4

# THE MIRACLE OF THE STUFF

## Healy, Alaska 1990

There were many things that occurred when we had our two house fires that demonstrated to me, that even during a tragedy God is there. We may never understand why sometimes he saves us FROM the fire, and sometimes he saves us IN the fire, but either way he is with us. This is just ONE of the things that happened during that time that showed me his love.

We had built a 16' x 16' cabin to live in "temporarily until our big cabin on the hill was completed. It was barely big enough for Ed and I and our three youngest children but that October, our son-in-law Pete got excited about building a cabin on our homestead for he and Kim and their two kids, Steven and Amanda. Meanwhile the four of them moved into our cabin "temporarily."

The cold weather and lots of early snowstorms caused them to put off the cabin building till spring, so we had an interesting winter with nine of us co-existing in a very small space.

One of the things that helped is that we built the beds on platforms just above our heads so we could use the space below. For instance, under one bed was the kitchen table.

Still it was crowded and to make matters worse I seem to be a collector of stuff. I kept my "stuff" in a curtained off area under our bed. I had pictures, and cards and stories I had written, things for craft projects I intended to learn to do and educational materials I had made since we homeschooled our kids.

Over the course of the winter and spring the others in the cabin would from time to time make derogatory comments about all "my stuff" and how much more room we would have without it. I usually ignored them but finally, that summer I had heard enough of their snide remarks and I got mad.

I went up the hill to the new building site and nailed a pole between two big birch trees and hung a tarp over the pole and staked it to the ground to make a tarp tent. I then drug a couple of pallets inside to help keep the boxes dry and proceeded to haul all my "stuff" up to the tent.

I was fuming for I knew besides possible weather damage there was also the squirrels and bears and other animals that tended to get into things left outside. Still I was determined to get all my "stuff" out of the cabin so everyone would stop complaining about it.

Just a couple of weeks later our cabin burned to the ground. Nothing was saved but Kerry's rifle which Ed grabbed going out the door and of course ALL my "Stuff!"

In retrospect, I am more inclined to believe God prompted everyone in the family to keep nagging me about "My stuff" to get me to move it out of there before the fire. Though it had very little monetary value, God knew that I wouldn't be crying over the basic household goods that burned up, but I would be saddened by my personal items and mementoes being destroyed. One of the things moved into the tent was my old prayer journal. Rereading it after the fire, and being reminded of all the things God had already seen us through, restored my faith and hope for the future.

A year later we had a better home and better stuff. I was reminded of Job's statement, "Naked came I out of my mother's womb, and naked shall I return thither: the LORD gave, and the LORD hath taken away; blessed be the name of the LORD." Job 1:21

My heart is fixed, O God,

my heart is fixed:

I will sing and give praise."

Psalm 57:7

# HERE—WILL THIS COVER IT?

## Healy, Alaska 1990

A few days after our first cabin burned to the ground I had gone up with my son Kody and raked the charred debris into a pile.

Kody, who was eight, kept digging things out of my debris pile, like the charred metal chair frame and telling me I could paint it and put a new seat on it, but I shook my head no. Then he drug out the extension cord I had tossed onto the pile because it had melted in two.

"We could put a new end on this, "he said.

"I don't want it—throw it away, "I replied.

"Boy—you sure are wasteful! "he declared.

Still as I raked and looked around the yard I found a few meager items that I deemed were not trash and I put them in a metal trash can with a lid to keep them dry. Believe me it was not much.

When we were done we walked the mile back over to our neighbors—the Smarts, where we were staying. The clean-up project had been both physically and emotionally draining.

About a week later Ed and I returned to the burn site only to discover a bear had been curious about the barrel and had tipped it over and strewn the contents all over, biting into or shredding whatever he could. It had also rained several times that week and now there appeared to be NOTHING worth salvaging.

I was unreasonably angry. Though what I had saved was of very little value—it was MY stuff! As we walked the three miles out to the road Ed tried to calm me down, but to no avail. We were headed to our school bus we had parked at a friend's house; we had been using it for storage and wanted to see what was in there that we could use.

Mostly it was impractical items for homestead living like an electric coffee pot, a curling iron and my china. Since all my plastic dishes had burned up we decided we would now use the china and my monogrammed silverware as well. I had to smile at that as we were temporarily living in a tiny 8'8' addition to the neighbor's horse barn that had a bed and a little wood stove in it. However the damage the bear had done to the few salvageable items by our cabin kept running through my mind like a broken record.

I was flipping through some books deciding which ones I wanted to take to read when out fell a crisp $100 dollar bill. I was speechless! The thought that immediately popped into my head from the Lord was, "Here, will that cover it?"

I know it was a direct communication from the Lord for at first I didn't get what he meant, but the thought came to me again and almost seemed a little sarcastic. Then I understood that he was talking about the junk I had saved in the trash can. If I would have sold everything in there I doubt I would have gotten $20. So the Lord gave me a $100 bill so I would shut up about it and let it go.

Of course someone might assume we had to have put the $100 in the book ourselves, but we had been getting by on so little for so long there is no way we would have ever stuck a hundred dollar bill inside a book and forgotten about it.

I had to learn to let go because God was up to something, as usual. When I finally could laugh about it and thank the Lord for the hundred dollars and let go of "MY STUFF," God opened the windows of heaven and poured out a blessing through the people of our community—most of whom we did not know.

They had a spaghetti feed in to raise money as well as took donations of clothes and furniture and household goods to replace what we had lost in the fire. Some people from the community also came up to help us finish the bigger cabin we had been working on when the small one burned down. Even some windows and doors were donated.

When we finally got settled in our new cabin and looked around I realized that the things we had been given were better than the things that had burned up—plus now we knew lots of wonderful people in our community that we might have never known if we had not had the fire.

God is generous. He does not just give us the essentials. He loves to surprise us. One day I was visiting a new friend I had made in town and we were talking about the fire. I told her I had a whole different perspective now. "The things you need are not the essentials," I said. "I never cried over the pans that burned up or the broom. All those kind of things can be replaced. But there are things I will miss."

"Like what? "She asked.

"Well pictures of course—and my mom gave me a canister set with rabbits in the woods on it," I sighed. Then as I described the bright colors and the detailed artwork she began to smile.

"Like these?" she asked coming back from her kitchen.

"Yes," I said surprised.

"You can take them," she said—"I am not using them. I have another canister set."

Of course you could say these blessings all happened because of people—not God, but I know that God often answers prayers by moving upon the hearts of people who are listening, even though often they think they got the idea all by themselves.

I realized I was a hoarder by nature and always feared lack. I didn't consider it a lack of trust to try to have everything I could possibly need for any and every situation we might face in life. God however was at work in me teaching me two lessons at once: Everything you can stockpile here on earth can be gone in an instant—AND God is able to supply you with every good thing as you need it if you will only trust in him and his goodness.

THE LORD GIVETH AND THE
LORD TAKETH AWAY,
BLESSED BE THE
NAME OF THE LORD
JOB 1:21

# GOD SPEAKS

## Healy, Alaska 1998

People forget that God is watching us all the time. We also tend to think that he doesn't get involved in the petty little details of our lives, but if you ask him you might be surprised to discover that he has been eavesdropping all the time and is very aware of your situation. This was one of those times when God spoke.

One day I got mad at Ed. Now I can't even remember what I was mad about. We had gone somewhere in the car and I remember I was giving him the silent treatment, I'm not sure that he wasn't enjoying it. I knew I couldn't keep it up as I was very aware of the scripture that said, "Let not the sun go down upon your wrath" Ephesians 4:26. We had always tried to follow that scriptural principle which meant that somehow we would have to make up before dark. However, I thought to myself smugly, it's early yet. I can be mad all day. Then I considered the fact that it was summertime in Alaska. The sun wouldn't be going down until about 2AM!

Now even though I can't remember WHY I was angry, doesn't mean I didn't have a very good reason at the time. I'm not the type to fly off the handle though I do admit I can have my feelings hurt easily. Regardless, it was all forgotten when God spoke.

Ed had gotten out of the car to take care of some errand and I was waiting in the car, still fuming. Our Bible was laying there on the seat for we always kept one with us. I glanced over it and sighed. "Lord do you have anything to say to me on this matter?" I asked aloud.

I reached over and flipped open the Bible randomly and pointed. Now I know there are many preachers who say this is not a good way to get a word from God but this is what I read: "Then said the LORD,

Doest thou well to be angry? Jonah 4:4. I stared at the verse and began to laugh. "Okay Lord, I'll let him off the hook and forgive him I guess."

Like I said, I sure wish I could remember what he had done because I am positive you would all think I was justified in being angry. However who can argue with the Lord, or refuse his advice? That would be plain stupid.

So when Ed got back in the car I said. "The Lord told me I should stop being angry with you, so I forgive you." And I handed him the Bible and showed him the verse the Lord had given me. We both had a good laugh and of course kissed and made up. Guess what? The return trip home was much more pleasant.

Then said the LORD,

Doest thou well to be angry?

Jonah 4:4

# THE HEAVY WEIGHT

### Valdez, Alaska 1998

It was a busy time for us. I was working forty hours a week as a community support specialist with Horizons and working on my teaching degree through Prince William Sound Community College, also full time. I did not have time to be sick. So I tried ignoring a bad cold I had and it settled into my chest.

I went to bed that night with the feeling of a heavy weight on my chest. My breathing felt shallow and labored. I probably should have gone to the doctor but it was after hours and we had no insurance. I was exhausted and just wanted to go to sleep, hoping I would feel better in the morning.

However as Ed lay listening to my breathing he grew more concerned and felt like the Lord was telling him to start praying for me or I wasn't going to make it. He immediately placed his hands on my chest and began calling out to God. I remember thinking how his prayer sounded so heartfelt and desperate.

Instantly I felt the weight lift from my chest and I felt fine, yet Ed prayed on and on, crying out to God. Finally I had to interrupt him. "You can stop now, the minute you started praying I got healed."

I wish all our prayers were answered instantly as that one was. I don't know why there is sometimes a long delay where we must instead, labor on in faith believing, but I do know we serve a good God. He has our best interests at heart and he does answer our prayers, just stay in faith.

AND THE PRAYER OF FAITH
SHALL SAVE THE SICK,
AND THE LORD
SHALL RAISE HIM UP;
AND IF HE HATH COMMITTED
SINS, THEY SHALL BE
FORGIVEN HIM.
JAMES 5:15

# ZIG-ZAGGING ON THE GLENNALLEN

## Valdez, Alaska 1999

Ed and I, our son Kody, and our daughter Kandi were making the 300 mile trip into Anchorage. I don't recall the month, only that the roads were snow packed. In Alaska, on the Glennallen highway, the fact that the roads were snow packed doesn't narrow it down much except it probably wasn't July.

Ed has done a lot of winter driving and feels pretty confident of his driving skills no matter what the road is like. (The passengers may be a little less confident.) Regardless he was blitzing along at the posted speed limit.

He came around the corner and there was a motor home with its front end over the shoulder of the road and its rear end out over the center line. Just past it a pick-up truck was side-ways with its nose in the other ditch and its rear end out on the road.

It did not look like there was any way we could go in between them on the narrow road, and I didn't see how we could help but hit one or the other. You only have a split second to react in such situations and both Ed and I called upon the only one who was capable of giving us any real help. "Oh Jesus—help us!" Ed said. I think my vocabulary was reduced to "Jesus!" but HE knew I desperately wanted HIS intervention.

The drivers and passengers watched with mouths agape as Ed tapped the breaks lightly which caused the rear end of our van to start to slide towards the motor home. He quickly gave a slight twitch and the van moved in the other direction towards the pickup. Somehow, we fishtailed our way between them when it absolutely looked like there was no room to do so. Then Ed corrected slightly back in the other direction and the van slid back out towards the center of the road where he managed to straighten out again.

Having zigzagged between the vehicles without touching either everyone started breathing again and released a sigh of relief. But Kody was all smiles and enthusiastically exclaimed, "That was cool Dad!"

In all thy ways
acknowledge him and
he shall direct thy paths.
Proverbs 3:6

# THE HAIL PRAYER

### June 2000, Trapper Creek Alaska

We had moved to Trapper Creek, Alaska in January of 2000 so Ed and I could complete our BA degrees in Elementary Education at the Matanuska-Susitna Community College between Palmer and Wasilla. Trapper Creek was also where I could do home health care for my good friend Robin Smeltzer and Ed could lead worship at Greater Grace Community Church, where her husband pastored. We completed our classes the end of May and as usual gardening was on my mind.

Another friend from Maine who was helping at the church at that time was Charleena Burns. We needed some lettuce and potatoes so I decided I would take her into Wasilla to show her around and have lunch. Anyone who knows me knows I should never be the tour guide as I have no sense of direction and am always getting lost. I couldn't find the Chinese restaurant I was looking for so we kept wandering around.

In actuality, God was guiding me to exactly where he wanted me. While we were driving around lost, I spotted a sign that said "lettuce and free potatoes." These were the only two items on my grocery list so we quickly turned in knowing it was a God thing.

There we discovered a little old lady selling vegetable starts for 50 cents a six pack and they were the best starts I had seen anywhere. Immediately was born in my heart the idea to start a community garden on the church property to keep the food bank they ran in fresh produce—something that is hard to have enough of in the outlying areas of Alaska.

She also happily gave us 400 pounds of free potatoes for the food bank and every other available space in the trunk and floorboards was filled with garden starts. We arrived home and Pastor Smeltzer got on the phone and found a volunteer to come plow up an old garden site.

Early Wednesday I started in planting. I worked in the garden all day, only quitting in time to wash up for the Wednesday night service. As we stood up to sing during the service it began to rain.

At first I was happy, thinking that was exactly what my new little transplants needed, a good watering. But then it began to rain very hard and I said to the Lord, "don't let it rain too hard on my garden or it will beat my baby plants down."

I had no sooner got the prayer out of my mouth when it started to rain even harder and the wind began to blow as well. I continued to pray and then I heard hail hitting the tin roof of our little log church. I wanted to run out to cover the garden but I didn't have anything to cover it with. The more I prayed the worse it seemed to get.

I actually felt a little annoyed at God. I told him, "Well Lord it is YOUR garden." (Notice I had called it MY garden in my first prayer) "I only planted it because I thought you wanted me too, but if you don't want me to start a community garden then I guess I'll do something else." The hail continued and I couldn't help thinking how all my hard work and planning had been for nothing.

About the time the service ended so did the hail. I put on my jacket and ran outside to see how much damage had been done. There was pea sized hail covering the lawn. There were big piles of it several inches deep where it had come off the roof. A tree in the lot next to the church had broken in half.

But as I got to the garden, I stood amazed. In wonderment I stared at the sign I had put up—TRAPPER CREEK COMMUNITY GARDEN. There was not even one piece of hail past that sign. I began to laugh. "You really got me going that time Lord!" So I went and got a big glass and filled it with the hail and poured my Pepsi in it. "A toast to you Lord!" It reminded me of the following verse that has been made into a song.

I know whom
I have believed in,
and am persuaded that he is
able to keep that
which I've committed unto
him until that day."
II Timothy 1:12

# THE FUR COAT INCIDENT

### Trapper Creek, Alaska 2000

God never ceases to amaze me! He is so kind, generous, merciful and thoughtful. He shows his love in many small ways that I think people often don't recognize. He leaves anonymous gifts for his children all the time but we do not always give him the credit. I purposely look for his handiwork; like the fur coat incident.

Our daughters, Katrina and Kim, our grandkids Steven and Amanda and daughter-in-law Courtney, all wanted us to meet them at the state fair in Palmer. It was before payday so we were down to rolling coins from our piggy bank but we wanted to spend some time with them before our student teaching started, so off we went.

We decided to concentrate on the free stuff like the animal barn and all the entries but when it started to rain and the wind began to blow, we opted for the heated building where all the vendors were selling things.

As we warmed up and browsed around I noticed a booth selling expensive fur coats by David Green furrier. I went over and tried one on that I especially liked and modeled it for Ed. We both thought it was beautiful but knew that we did not have the money to buy a coat like that, and even if we could afford it, we would never spend the $3000 or more for a coat. So I gave it one last hug and hung it back on the rack. The saleswoman, obviously not knowing our financial position, handed Ed their business card, which he pocketed, thinking no more about it.

On Sunday, I got up early since I usually volunteered by keeping the clothes in the free clothes room of our church in order and I knew it was getting pretty messy. After I matched shoes and hung clothes for about an hour, I was down to the last bag donated to the clothing exchange.

*Donna Varnes*

Imagine my surprise when I dumped out a fur coat from David Green's furrier that was very similar to the one I had admired and modeled. Of course it just happened to also be in my size! A coincidence?—I think not! I ran and got my winter coat and happily exchanged it for my new fur coat. But I am not telling everyone about my coat—you remember what happened to Joseph!

Not that I speak in
respect of want:
for I have learned,
in whatsoever state I am
therewith to be content.
Philippians 4:11

# THE GREAT PHYCIAN MAKES A NIGHT CALL

### Trapper Creek, Alaska 2001

We were at a very busy time in our lives. We were doing our student teaching in Talkeetna, AK and I was working, plus we were very involved in our church.

I didn't have time to get sick so I kept ignoring the sore throat I had. My tongue also got coated and sore. As the weeks passed instead of getting better I felt sicker and sicker. My tongue developed lesions that bled and it was very painful to swallow.

We had no extra money so I hated to run up a bill for a doctor and a prescription. Instead I cried out to the Great Physician. "What in the world do I have to do Lord?" I asked. "And what should I do?" I had of course been praying about this all along, but on that night I got a house call.

Oh it was not Jesus in person or an angel, but in the form of a dream. In my dream I went to the doctor. The doctor looked in my mouth and said, "You have thrush." Then I woke up. I sat up and thought about the dream. *Thrush?—isn't that just something babies get? I asked myself.*

I got up and went on the internet and looked up thrush and it described my symptoms perfectly. For thrush that did not clear up on its own you needed a prescription. *"Well I can't do that Lord,"* I said.

Immediately the thought popped into my head—*you have tea tree oil—why don't you gargle with it? But tea tree oil is very strong,* I argued. It *did get rid of the fungus on my feet but is it safe to gargle with?*

Then I considered the fact that I would never have diagnosed myself with thrush, nor would I have considered using tea tree oil in my mouth as I had always thought of it as something strictly for external use, therefore these thoughts had to have come from the Lord.

I put two or three drops of tea tree oil in a glass of water and began gargling with it several times a day. The next day I was better and by day three all symptoms were gone. Thank you Lord for making that house call!

Note: Sometimes the Lord heals instantly. We have had many examples of this in our own lives as well as in the Bible. However God chose many different ways to heal in the Bible. Hezekiah was simply told he would recover. One prophet had to lay stretched out on a dead child three times before he was healed. Naaman was told to go dunk himself in the Jordan River seven times to be healed, and Jesus himself once put mud on a blind man's eyes to restore his eyesight. The point is we cannot and must not try to put God in a box. We need to be open to hearing from him and doing what he says and waiting patiently and expectantly for our miracle to come.

Katrina, Kandi, Kim, Kerry, Donna, Ed, Courtney, Kody
At Kerry and Sully's wedding 2003

# DEGENREATIVE DISC DISEASE REVERSED

## Mekoryuk, Alaska 2001

We were teaching school in the village of Meroryuk on Nunivac Island, in the Bering Sea, off the west coast of Alaska. It was lunch break and Ed and I had walked to the teacher housing to eat. I made two lattes, one for me and one to take back to Lanay Raines, who was the principal at the time.

Though it was April, we were still having winter like weather. The metal steps outside our apartment were icy and as I stepped down with a latte in each hand, I slipped and fell hard on the steps. Though I cried out in pain, I had to laugh that I was holding my lattes upright and hadn't spilled either one.

As Ed took them from me and attempted to help me up, I realized I couldn't move, and any slight attempt at movement caused excruciating pain. Ed left me then and went to get help. He prayed to God that I hadn't broken my back.

There was a medical clinic in the village, but no doctors, only some health aides. To get me there was another problem. There were few vehicles other than snow machines in the village, except for the pick-up that belonged to the school. Soon the pick-up arrived with some of the high school boys who put me on a stretcher and lifted me into the back of the pick-up. The back of the pick-up was about half filled with snow so the ride over to the clinic was quite cold.

Once inside, the health aides did their best to check me over. They were on the phone to a doctor in Bethel and it was determined I needed to be flown to the hospital there. The only thing I could do was lay there on the stretcher, on the floor of the medical clinic and wait for the plane to arrive. This took several hours.

Once it arrived, the high-schoolers again picked me up on the stretcher and placed me in the back of the pick-up for the five mile drive to the gravel landing strip. By the time I was transported into the plane, my teeth were chattering.

It took over six hours from the time of the accident till I arrived at the hospital. Once there, the x-rays determined that thankfully, nothing was broken. Still I could not move. I was given pain killers and an anti-inflammatory but it only seemed to make a difference if I lay perfectly still. Any attempt at movement caused excruciating pain.

This began my months of pain medications and therapy. I wanted to be treated by a doctor I knew and trusted, so I flew several times to Valdez and Anchorage for treatment. Ed had to push me through the airports and wherever we went in a wheel chair, and I carried my pillow with me everywhere as it was just too uncomfortable to sit.

When the doctors representing the insurance company examined me, they said that the reason the fall had caused so much pain and damage was because I already had degenerative disc disease. There was no cure for that; they predicted it would just slowly get worse.

The school was very supportive. Therefore, I was able to work as many hours a day as I could with an aide to help me, and used up my sick leave for the times I couldn't.

I started out taking a few medications, but due to side-effects from those medications, they kept adding another medication. One day I realized I was up to eight prescription drugs and I thought "this is crazy. I'm not going to live like this."

I started to cut back on them all and soon I was only taking a pain medication occasionally if I couldn't stand it anymore. Through it all we were of course praying for my healing but it seemed elusive, sometimes feeling better, sometimes worse.

For the next several years the pain was always in the background. I would go forward for prayer at various churches from time to time and have them pray for my back. Often the pain would leave and I would marvel at how good it felt to be pain-free. But then, sooner or later it would begin hurting again.

We had moved to the lower 48 when our parents started having serious health issues. After Ed's mom passed away, he got a job driving a semi-truck all over the USA. I was a professional passenger. Besides having air-ride seats, I could stretch out on the bunk whenever I needed to. However it seemed as though my back was hurting less and less.

We had insurance again so I started going to a chiropractor. I said, "The insurance company doctors claimed I have degenerative disc disease, but perhaps they were just trying to get out of paying as much for the settlement. It seems to be bothering me less and less."

So he took x-rays and hung them up for me to see. "You definitely have degenerative disc disease," he said pointing out all the things wrong with my spine. Eventually these discs will probably fuse together, the only thing you can do is come in for treatment about three times a week to try to keep your mobility."

Unfortunately the insurance had a cap on it and once it was exhausted I couldn't afford to go for treatment three times a week indefinitely. I went as often as I could, but while on the road that wasn't often. Still, instead of getting worse as had been predicted, my back continued to bother me less and less often. Today, nine years later I rarely have a problem with my back. Perhaps if I went in to have it x-rayed it would show the Lord had healed it completely, or perhaps it would show it had fused together after-all. Regardless of the doctor's report, God has the final say. He also left us many promises in his Word, as in Exodus 15:27 "for I am the LORD that healeth thee."

That is true whether the healing is instantaneous or a slow process. Just considering how marvelously he created our bodies to heal and repair themselves, is in itself a miraculous thing. When he steps in and makes things that are naturally supposed to get worse and worse, and instead they get better and better, we give Him all the praise and glory.

A MERRY HEART
DOETH GOOD LIKE A MEDICINE,
BUT A BROKEN SPIRIT
DRIETH THE BONES.
PROVERBS 17:22

# JEFF'S DOG

## Yachats, Oregon 2006

Every summer we try to take at least one of our grandkids on a summer trip with us. It is how we get to know their likes and dislikes and spend some quality time together. This summer we had nine year-old Kyrsten with us, and we hoped to show her a good time as well as help her to get reacquainted with relatives she seldom got to see.

We drove from Idaho to Portland, Oregon where Ed's brother and family live and then down the coast to Yachats to see his cousins, the Lee's. When we arrived everyone seemed a little emotional and we knew something was wrong.

"What's the matter," I asked Charleen.

"Well, Jeff's dog that he has had forever can't get up any more. She's an old dog and we called the vet and they recommended we put her to sleep, so we have an appointment in the morning to take her in."

About that time Jeff came in and I said, "I'm sorry about your dog Jeff, can we pray for her?"

"Yeah—go ahead."

"Kyrsten do you want to go pray for Jeff's dog with me?"

"Sure."

So we went over to where the dog was lying in the sun looking almost dead already. Her coat was dull and her eyes sad. We laid our hands on her and prayed for her to recover and have life and vitality.

We only had time for lunch and a short visit before we had to head on down the coast to California where more of Kyrsten's cousins lived. The next day I almost dreaded calling. What if they had gone ahead and put the dog to sleep as planned. Kyrsten would be heart-broken. But I got up my nerve and called. "So how'd things go concerning the dog?" I asked.

"Well, funny thing is when Jeff got up in the morning to take the dog in to be put to sleep, she was up walking around the yard and seemed fine, so he canceled her appointment."

"Wow—we're so glad to hear that!" and I related the good news to Kyrsten and Ed. But that is not the end of the story.

Ed and I made a trip back through in 2009 and the dog was out in the yard sunning herself again. But this time she got up when we came and was wagging her tail. She looked so much younger and healthier than the last time we saw her. Her eyes were bright and her coat shiny. It was such a transformation I turned to Jeff and asked, is this the same old dog we prayed for last time we were here?"

"Yes, that's her"

"Well the dog looks like she is doing better than you—I think maybe we should pray for you this time," and we all laughed. Of course all our family and friends know they are all in our thoughts and prayers always.

Let every thing
That hath breath
Praise the Lord.
Psalm 150:6

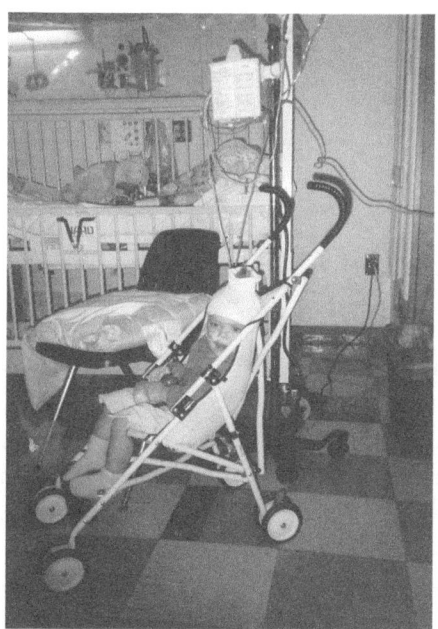

Crystal in the hospital

Crystal and her Daddy, Kevin, ready for church, first Sunday home

# LEARNING SPIRITUAL WARFARE

## Skiatook, Oklahoma September 2006

We had dropped what we were doing to step in and help my oldest son, Kevin, take care of his four children after his wife left him. He was gone out of town a lot team driving nationwide with my husband. We had been trying to buy a home and the deal had fallen through and we needed to move to another house. I was used to having my capable, outgoing husband Ed around to help me in the many areas I felt uncomfortable in dealing with, but now it seemed I was on my own. At just this vulnerable time we got a call that rocked us.

Kevin had an 18 month old daughter, Crystal, who was born after his wife left him. Since Kevin suspected she was in an unsafe environment he had been trying to get custody of her. I even had a vivid dream that I was putting her in her car seat in our van and she was smiling up at me. I was puzzled when authorities didn't act on Kevin's concerns. Now here was the call that exceeded our own worst fears.

Crystal had been shook and thrown by the boyfriend who had been babysitting her.

She was on life-support in a coma. Her prognosis looked bleak. All the air seemed to have gone from my body.

I hung up the phone. I had already sent Kevin's other four kids off on the bus and stood there alone. It was just too much. All I wanted to do was retreat to my room, crawl in bed and cry. I headed down the hall.

Just then I heard the voice of God in my spirit say clearly, "I don't want you to retreat—I want you to attack!" That certainly wasn't something I would think.

Anyone who knows me would certainly question God giving a command like that to me. I avoid even minor conflict. I leave the room if someone starts to raise their voice. I certainly didn't like to fight or argue and had never "attacked" anyone. Yet God had already been dealing with me on this issue. I had always sighed and "wished" Satan would leave our family and church alone but had never really put up a good fight. I didn't know where to start. But I had had a dream months earlier that was still on my mind.

*My family and I were in a theme park riding in cable cars having fun, but there were demon like creatures peering around rocks along our route and they had spears and arrows. We were laughing and having a good time thinking they were just part of the act. When they started shooting arrows at us, we jokingly started shooting back at them with the guns that had been provided but I wasn't really aiming, my intent was not to harm them. But in the dream the Lord spoke to me and said, "Shoot to kill! If you don't, they are going to destroy your family." And then I woke up.*

So here again God was telling me to "attack—shoot to kill." I went in my room and got a picture of my beautiful little blond-haired, blue-eyed, granddaughter. I lit a candle by it symbolizing my prayers going up to God.

I went to get my Bible in the living room, and when I walked in the room Joyce Meyer was on the television and she said, "We can't just sit around wishing Satan would leave us alone—we've got to engage in spiritual warfare." She described how Jesus had dealt with Satan by saying "It is written." So I sat down to listen as she gave powerful verse after verse. "Resist the Devil and he will flee from you." "We wrestle not against flesh and blood, but against principalities, and powers, and rulers of darkness of this world. Greater is he that is in you than he that is in the world." I started writing them all down on my sticky pad. Then I thought of some other promises I knew. "No good thing will he withhold from them that walk uprightly. I am the God that healeth thee,"—and others.

I went around the house and stuck the verses wherever I would see them the most, over the light switches, above the sink. And over the next few days I kept adding verses till I had over 60 plastered in every conceivable place. As I saw them I read them out loud and prayed. I put worship music on at one end of the house and Christian preaching on at the other end of the house, so that no matter where I was working I was hearing the Word and praise. I needed all the spiritual encouragement I could get. I called all my Christian friends to pray. I added Crystal's name to every prayer chain I knew of.

I wanted to make Satan and his demonic friends as miserable as possible. I filled their ears with worship, prayers and praise and yelled my Bible verses out to him just to remind him who was over all, and all powerful. And I did get his attention.

I had even come up with a chorus I loved singing, "Satan, you're a loser, you're a liar, and you're going down!" I was singing it as I walked into the office. I was going to sit down in the office chair and look for some more promises of God. As I went to sit down, someone shoved me out of the chair onto the floor. Startled I whipped around to see who had shoved me, but there was no one there. Then it dawned on me that I had gotten under Satan's skin and he, or some demonic force had shoved me.

The reality of having an actual supernatural encounter with the other kingdom momentarily stunned me. Then the story of Job popped into my mind, and the fact that Satan had had to get permission to harm Job. I started laughing, now bold in my counter attack. "Is that all you could get permission to do?" I yelled. I was actually getting to him. He was actually noticing all my praise and worship and quoting of scripture, and it was making him mad! I was overjoyed! I was encouraged! I was on the right track! This elation I felt was despite the fact we still didn't know how Crystal was or what the outcome would be.

Though my son had left immediately to pick up her other grandparents and drive to the hospital in another state, when they arrived they wouldn't let anyone in her room till it was cleared by the court since it was now a criminal case.

His first glimpse of her was heartbreaking. Crystal was on life support and unresponsive. She had seizures. But as we kept up our prayer vigil she eventually came out of her coma. For several weeks Kevin stayed at her bedside trying to comfort and assure her despite the tubes, wires and machines. She no longer had the ability to sit up, stand, crawl, walk, talk or even eat as she had been able to do before. She was completely paralyzed on the right side.

Kevin finally did get custody and when she was well enough to move she was transferred to the hospital 20 miles from where we lived that had a doctor who specialized in shaken baby syndrome cases.

Crystal seemed frightened and cried whenever a doctor or nurse entered the room. We vowed to have someone with her around the clock to help comfort and encourage her. This began the many days spent at the hospital, while still trying to attend to the needs of the other four children.

Her broken arm was in a cast, she was still on a feeding tube, and I'm sure—did not understand why her mother wasn't there. After days of this I was wondering just how long we could keep this routine up. Everyone could not just stop working indefinitely. Our church held us all up in prayer. Sometimes I felt I could barely hang on till the next church meeting. The encouragement we got there kept us all going.

To the family, who were hoping for an instantaneous healing—her recovery seemed depressingly slow. The doctors however were amazed at her progress. We propped her up and took her for wagon rides in the hall pulling her IV pole along with us. She seemed determined to learn to walk again. We would hold her up as she attempted to drag her paralyzed leg along in an effort to take steps.

When we took her to the playroom, instead of enjoying the toys she could play with, she was obsessed with the big red plastic riding car they had. She would cry in frustration that she no longer had the ability to open the door and get inside. She struggled to make her body move as it should. Despite the cast on her arm and useless leg, through sheer determination and lots of twisting, turning, pulling, and tears, she would finally manage to get inside. She did not want help. She would sit there a few moments with a satisfied look on her face and then she would struggle to get out just so she could try to get back in. It was an endless fight and challenge for her—one which she would not give up on.

Generally the doctor came in the mornings while she was still in bed, and she always covered up her head with her blanket and cried whenever any doctor or nurse entered the room, so I don't think he realized just how much time she spent out of her room working on her self-prescribed physical therapy. She endlessly wanted to try to crawl up steps or walk with help.

When I mentioned to the doctor about her determination he seemed surprised. He was thinking she should be resting quietly as much as possible. I explained how bored she got in her room and how if she didn't get to go for her walks she got almost hysterical, and that we could only sing and do itsy bitsy spider for so long. He asked if she was singing along and I said she was.

Puzzled he asked me to come with him, that there was something he wanted me to see. We went over to his computer and he brought up the images of Crystal's brain. One side was full of little wrinkles and one side looked nearly blank. It was also somewhat smaller than the other side and detached from the skull. Even with my untrained eye I could see there was a problem.

"What is the damaged part in control of," I asked.

"Her movement, her speech and it even affects her digestion."

"But she has definitely been moving and talking, more every day," I replied.

"Yes—well I'm just showing you what I'm looking at."

Crystal seemed so upset with her hospital environment that we wondered if we could make arrangements for her to come home for a visit on the weekend when they scheduled fewer tests and therapies, so we asked the doctor about the possibility.

"Oh, no! She can't leave the hospital any time soon, even for the afternoon. Ask me again in about a month."

We were quite taken aback. She had already been in the hospital a month; we had somehow imagined she would be coming home soon. Still we kept pouring on the prayer, and just one week later the doctor said, "We've been going over all her charts and tests and decided we can release her from the hospital tomorrow as long as you are willing to bring her in for her physical therapy and other appointments."

This was only one week after the doctor had told us to ask him again about a home visit in a month!

Everyone was rejoicing and misty-eyed the day we took little Crystal to church for the first time. Though seemingly scared of all the people in the hospital, she smiled radiantly at everyone at church as if she had known them forever. She beamed and seemed at home and loved the worship music.

Though there were many, many appointments I had to take her to—eye specialists for the blood in her eyes, speech therapists, physical therapists, child development specialists—each one soon determined she had miraculously recovered. Eventually she was taken off her seizure medications as well with no problems.

Then one sunny day as I was buckling her into her car seat in our van, she looked up at me and gave me a big smile. I remembered my dream then, where I had seen her doing just that, and realized we had foiled Satan's plan in this little girl's life. Crystal loved church and loved to sing, and I wondered just what great things were in store for her. Since then I have not stopped "resisting the devil" and praising God who is faithful.

Jesus said,
Let the little children
come to me,
and do not hinder them,
for the kingdom of heaven
belongs to such as these.
Matthew 19:14

# THE COCKROACH PRAYER

## Calera, Oklahoma 2006

I was riding on the truck with Ed and was happy to discover we were routed through the town of Calera, Oklahoma where our friend Sue and her son Josh lived. I called Sue and she invited us to spend the night if we could. Ed planned it so we could take our mandatory 10-hour rest there.

They lived in a small older two bedroom home so we fully expected to sleep on our air mattress in the living room. However when we arrived we discovered that they had been cooking and cleaning and rearranging, and fully intended us to sleep in the master bedroom and Sue was going to sleep on the couch.

Her son Josh had fixed one of Ed's favorite meals—taco's. While we were eating Sue told us about the cockroach problem they were having and that they were intending to have the house sprayed on payday. Indeed, despite the kitchen being spotless, we couldn't help noticing every time one scurried across the floor or counter. We all tried to make sure they did not make it to their intended destination.

Ed and I decided right then that we would not be bringing our suitcases in as we did not want any stow-a-ways. Still we didn't want to miss out on the chance to visit so we were determined to stay as planned.

I killed several of the horrid things when I went into the bathroom. They seemed to be everywhere. As usual, Ed went on into bed while Sue, Josh and I stayed up drinking coffee till we were too tired to talk.

When I finally went to get into bed I killed a cockroach on the nightstand. Dare I turn off the light and go to sleep? The idea of a cockroach crawling across me while I slept really grossed me out. I tried closing my eyes several times but kept setting up looking around to ensure there were no cockroaches on the bed.

I was truly exhausted by this time. Suddenly a verse popped into my mind. Genesis1:26 "And God said, Let us make man in our image, after our likeness: and let them have dominion over the fish of the sea, and over the fowl of the air, and over the cattle, and over all the earth, and over every creeping thing that creepeth upon the earth." Surely the creepy things included cockroaches. I was supposed to have dominion over them. God said so.

Trying not to wake up Ed I got up and went into the bathroom where I spotted several cockroaches fleeing for cover. I announced to them as loud as I dared without waking anyone up, "In the name of Jesus, all of you cockroaches must leave this house immediately!" I smashed the one by the sink for emphasis. Then I quietly prayed over the entire house using all the other scripture ammunition I could think of—"no good thing will he withhold from them that walk uprightly" Psalms 84:11, and "whatsoever ye shall ask in my name, that will I do, that the Father may be glorified in the Son" John 14:13 as well as others.

Finally I went back to my room to crawl into bed. I looked over at the nightstand—no cockroach. I closed my eyes for a few minutes and looked again—no cockroaches. Then I drifted off to sleep.

Early the next morning I went into the bathroom and flipped on the light—no cockroaches! I hurried into the kitchen and looked around—no cockroaches. I started to laugh.

Sue woke up and asked me what I was laughing about and I explained to her my cockroach prayer. She had to get up and look around for herself. No cockroaches! Soon everyone was awake and noticing that the cockroaches had hit the road.

After we had breakfast and were getting ready to leave I said, "Well Sue, the Lord made the cockroaches leave, but now it's up to you to make sure they don't think they can come back." I have learned that God always honors his word when we take him at his word.

And God said,
Let us make man in our image,
after our likeness:
and let them have dominion
over the fish of the sea,
and over the fowl of the air,
over the cattle,
and over all the earth,
and over every creeping
thing . . .

Genesis 1:26

# THE CHRISTMAS DRESS

### Oxnard, California December 2006

It was almost Christmas and Ed was still trucking. We got a load for California so we planned to take our mandatory 34 hour rest there and go to church with our three children and their families living in the area. Not having an extensive wardrobe on the truck, I had Ed stop at a thrift store so I could find a dress to wear for the Christmas service. Since he couldn't afford much down time I was happy to find one I liked at the first stop for just a few dollars. When I got back in the truck Ed hung it up between the bunk and the cupboard so it would not get wrinkled.

Things went as planned and we were able to spend the night with Kody, Courtney, and our two year old granddaughter Stephanie. When we got up in the morning I had Ed bring in the dress and I put it on. I came out into the living room to show Kody and Courtney the dress and it was then we discovered that somehow, while hanging in the truck it had gotten damaged and now had black streaks all over one side. They would not wash off. I was reminded of the verse referring to Satan which says: "The thief does not come except to steal, and to kill, and to destroy," John 10:10. I felt Satan had something to do with my dress getting ruined, after we had carefully hung it up, and I was mad.

Remembering the Scripture in Proverbs 6:30-31 which says "a thief . . . when he is found, he must restore sevenfold," I shouted out loud, "Okay Satan, you may have ruined my Christmas dress, but I'm asking God—the righteous judge, to make you give me another one—a better one—a NEW one, in return!"

So I put on some pants and went to church. We had a great service and afterward we were all invited to have lunch with my son Kerry at his in-laws house. When we got there, his mother-in-law Elena, handed me a package. I was surprised as we had drawn names for gifts this year and I knew she had not drawn mine.

"Yes, but when I saw it I thought of you and just had to get it," she said.

I opened the box and started to laugh. There was a dress—a better dress—a NEW dress! As I hugged her I explained why I was laughing. I had to wait only two hours for God to restore to me what the enemy had taken.

Therefore will I give thanks
unto thee O Lord, and sing
praises unto thy name
Psalms 18:49

The angel my dad, Jack placed in the garden 2006

# THE ANGEL SURPRISE

## Gillette, WY Summer 2006

Ed and I had been driving across the nation for months, sleeping in our semi-truck which was becoming more and more crowded. I never learned the art of packing light so despite our small quarters I had a complete office, my laptop, my printer/scanner, a minimum of ten books, some scrap booking supplies and mementoes I had picked up along the way including a collection of rocks and pressed flowers. Usually the items I considered buying were small in consideration of Ed.

On this rainy day however, we were doing our power walk inside a Home Depot. I called it my power shopping since I kept up our fast walking pace yet still managed to look at everything on display. It was then I spotted an angel in the garden department that was about 36 inches tall. I fell in love with her and she was also on sale for a great price so I REALLY wanted to buy her.

Ed usually humors me and doesn't complain about the things I buy but a large statue of an angel that belongs outdoors in a yard was not an item he thought we needed in the truck. He reasoned with me during each lap. "Why don't you wait till we have a place to put the thing? I don't want to move it off our bunk every time I want to go to sleep. We don't have a house, where would you put it?"

"We could take it to moms and put it in her new rock garden," I suggested. "It would look great there and I could see it whenever we visited." Still I couldn't convince him.

"We have no idea when we will get a load to Gillette. We might have to haul that angel around for months," he argued. So in the end we left without the angel. God however, who loves us all extravagantly, planned a little surprise for me.

*Donna Varnes*

It was a month or two before we got a load close enough to stop in at my moms, but when we drove into the yard, to my surprise and delight—there was the angel I had wanted to buy, standing in the middle of mom's new rock garden—exactly where I had intended to put it.

After hugs and greetings I asked about the angel. I was surprised that it was not my mom, but my dad Jack who saw the angel in town one day and decided to buy it. He was completely unaware that I had wanted it. And he just happened to put it where I had envisioned it standing. I of course think God instigated the whole thing just to delight me, just as any father likes to do for his children.

Delight thyself in the Lord
and He will give you
the desires of thy heart.

Psalms 37:4

# MY TWENTY DOLLAR ALLOWANCE FROM THE LORD

## Skiatook, Oklahoma 2007

Have you ever felt certain that something miraculous had happened but knew you could never prove it to others? Well this is one of those instances.

Because I tend to be careless with my purse I don't like to carry around a lot of money, however I hate to be broke. I told Ed once I would be happy as long as he made sure I always had a twenty dollar bill in my pocket. It became a sort of joke.

Every payday Ed would hand me my twenty and I would put it in my wallet. Whenever it was gone I would let him know I needed another. This was not grocery or bill paying money it was just my spending money.

We had been doing this for quite some time. Then he started team driving with our oldest son Kevin. It often worked out that they were out of town when my twenty ran out. When it did I always felt a wave of sadness. Oh it wasn't really about the $20; it just reminded me how much I missed him. I was struck by this feeling that I was completely on my own. However irrational it was I felt a sense of abandonment.

Where was Ed who constantly did little things to show me he loved me? Where was Ed who always encouraged and supported me? But I was never really abandoned. Someone was always looking out for me. Someone else was always trying to encourage me.

Something mysterious kept happening time and time again. Whenever I would look in my wallet and sigh because Ed wasn't there to do the ritual of replenishing my $20, that same day I would be doing laundry, or reach into a coat pocket or drawer and discover a twenty dollar bill. It was always a twenty dollar bill and it was always one I was certain I had not put there. I believe it was God.

God often does little things just to show us he loves us. Many people just miss them because they can't seem to believe and don't expectantly look for them.

In God we boast
all the day long,
and praise thy name forever.

Psalm 44:8

# SLEEPING IN TORNADO ALLEY

### Tulsa, Oklahoma 2008

We had lived in what's considered tornado alley, in the 70's and again from 2005-2008. During that time we must have prayed our way through storms hundreds of times. This then is just another example.

Ed had been doing over the road trucking since 2004 and usually put in 70 plus hours a week. So when his truck needed to go into the shop we decided to take the opportunity to rent a motel in Tulsa. We talked about how we would sit in the sauna, use the exercise room and kick back and watch movies all night.

However, in less than 20 minutes after we checked in, Ed had fallen fast asleep. *Oh well,* I thought, *I'll just watch old mushy movies that only I like.* So I started flipping channels. I settled on a movie and a back-up show to watch during commercials and was checking my email on my laptop.

Then my program was interrupted by a severe thunderstorm watch. It seems there were two different storm fronts heading our way. I was glad we wouldn't have to be out driving in it. But as the evening progressed they started talking about the possibility of some tornadoes heading our way. Then the tornado watch turned into an actual tornado warning.

Now I hadn't been particularly paying attention when Ed drove to our motel and I wasn't quite sure what part of town we were in, but as I watched the progress of the two storm fronts, one southwest of Tulsa, moving northeast, and the other northwest of Tulsa moving southeast, I didn't see how they could possibly miss our location. It looked like it was a good time to start praying.

I was even considering waking up Ed. On the one hand—where would we go if I did wake him? But then how would I feel if a tornado hit us and I had to tell Ed, "I would have warned you but I didn't want to wake you." I didn't have to debate this very long however, as Ed's eyes popped open and he looked around, as if to see where he was.

Relieved I said, "Ed, look at the television. It looks like a couple tornadoes are headed right for us."

Ed sat bolt upright and exclaimed "Really?" He listened to the forecaster for a few brief moments and then I realized he had fallen back to sleep.

It was just like Ed to be able to sleep through a tornado warning, trusting that God was watching out for us. It appeared I probably couldn't talk him into getting up and finding out where the nearest tornado shelter was located either. And now at 2AM in the morning there was nothing worth watching on television either, so I prayed "Lord, watch over and protect us, and turn the storms away, and help me sleep as peacefully as Ed." So I turned off the lights, laptop and T.V. and went to sleep.

When I woke up in the morning I could see the sun streaming through the crack in the curtains. I got up and looked out the window to see a gloriously sunny day, though the pavement was still wet from rain. Everything looked clean and fresh.

I turned on the local news. Sure enough, they were recounting how one storm had turned and gone further south, and how the other storm had just dissipated, so that both storms missed Tulsa altogether except for the rain. How many times does God do things like this on the behalf of someone's prayers? And how often do we take the time to thank him?

I will both lie down
in peace, and sleep;
for You alone,
O Lord,
make me dwell in safety.

Psalm 4:8

# THE WEDDING BLESSING

### Oxnard, California 2008

My daughter Katrina had been going with Nick for a year or so when they got engaged. He was the type who worked hard, had a savings and retirement fund and very little debt. My daughter on the other hand tended to buy whatever she wanted and was very generous where her friends and family were concerned and didn't have an actual budget. Isn't it interesting how God always seems to bring opposites together to temper them both.

Anyway as they began sharing their hopes and dreams and finances, Nick began to work with Katrina to get all her credit cards paid off and set up a fund for their wedding. He even put most of her bills on his own credit cards as he had a much lower interest rate. They now had a budget.

They planned their wedding far enough out so they had time to get the credit card debts under control and there was sufficient money in the wedding fund to pay for everything. He did not want to charge anything.

So when I arrived in California to help with wedding preparations, and Katrina confided in me that they were over-budget and there were still a lot of things to pay for I raised my eyes. I suggested she cut something out of her plans.

"I can't," she said. It's things I have already ordered that I have to pay for, like the cake and the chairs and dishes we are renting for the reception."

"Well how much are you short?"

"About $500. I am going to have to put it on my credit card."

Having just paid for our trip down, new outfits and getting my hair done, we were in no position to come up with that kind of money and I didn't think anyone else in the family could either. But I knew I didn't want her to start off her wedding on the wrong foot by running up the credit cards that he had just consolidated with his own.

So of course I took up the problem with my heavenly Father. "Lord please bless Katrina and Nick by sending some extra money from an unexpected source so she can cover these expenses, she needs" . . . and I stopped and thought, *let's ask for a little extra*—"a thousand dollars. Thank you."

My daughter worked as a personal trainer at the time, and was taking some time off for their wedding and honeymoon. So on the last day of work as she was saying her goodbyes to everyone, one of her clients handed her a card. She thanked him but thought she would wait to open it with Nick.

Nick and I were at the apartment when she opened the card, and started screaming. We were all wondering what in the world she was so excited about, until she showed us the enclosed check for $1000.00—from I might add, a completely unexpected source!

Who can utter the mighty acts Of the Lord? Who can show forth all his praise?

Psalm 106:2

# THE FORGOTTEN PURSE

### Houston, Texas February 3, 2008

Ed had a load to deliver in Houston, Texas so we hoped to go to Joel Osteen's church (Lakeside) that Sunday. We took a cab as we doubted there would be parking for our semi-truck. It was an awesome service!

Afterwards, we decided to do some exploring, so we took off walking. We came across a small but very busy café (always a good sign) and went inside. There was a man playing music so we took a booth close by thanking the Lord for our good seats.

After eating, Ed and I crossed the freeway and headed for a little strip mall in the distance. We had been gone from the café for about two hours when I suddenly realized I no longer had my purse.

Leaving your purse in a busy café in downtown Houston for a couple hours generally meant you were out a purse—but we prayed and hurried back to the café. When we entered we could see my purse, still sitting in plain sight, at the best seat in the place—untouched. God watches over us and our stuff!

Casting all your care

Upon him;

For he careth for you

1 Peter 5:7

# THE FORGOTTEN KEYS

## Southwest USA 2008

One day I came to the conclusion I was wasting too much time and frustration looking for lost things. I decided to start praying that God would just have the lost things turn up. I already knew that God usually just puts a thought in your head where to look, but sometimes he goes way beyond the natural to answer these kinds of prayer, as he did in this instance.

It happened during the time Ed was driving semi-truck all across the nation and I was riding with him. We had stopped at a truck stop to shower and do laundry so we came back to the truck with our arms loaded down with laundry, shower bags and drinks. Ed always left one key in the truck and carried a spare in his pocket, so he used his spare to unlock the door for me. Once open he decided to throw the laundry up on my seat and climb in from my side. When he did so he dropped the key on the ground. He knew he dropped it and fully intended to step back out and pick the key up as soon as he moved the bags out of my way. I hadn't noticed the dropped key and climbed in after him and handed him his drink. Ed got side tracked putting it in the tray and just slipped into his seat and drove off.

We had gone about 50 miles when Ed remembered he had forgotten to go back out to pick up his spare key from off the ground, and he was especially upset because it was attached to a little green tractor key chain that he liked. But it was not worth the fuel and time to go back to get so we just drove on.

A couple weeks later as we were having our morning Bible reading and prayer, I added "Please return all lost things to us Lord." I was not even thinking about the key Ed had dropped, it was just a general prayer.

*Donna Varnes*

We were many miles away from that dropped key by this time and had forgotten all about it. But God hadn't.

When we jumped up the next morning Ed unplugged his cell phone from the charger and went to set it in the cup holder where he had been putting it every morning, but today it wouldn't fit down inside like it always did. Ed was stunned when he looked to see what the problem was. There was his spare key he had dropped and the green tractor attached to the key was big enough to keep the phone from fitting in the holder right. It could not have been there before as he had been using this spot for his phone every day—it couldn't have gone unnoticed for two weeks! The only explanation was that when I prayed that simple prayer—God sent an angel to go fetch it for us and put it where we were sure to notice it! We serve an awesome God who cares about what we care about and pays attention to what we say.

Sing to Him,

Sing psalms to Him;

Talk of all

His wondrous works!

Psalm 105:2

# THE TEETH PRAYER

### Butte, Montana 2009

I know when I start talking about finding things after I have prayed that there are many skeptics who can think of hundreds of things that they have misplaced that they later found without any heavenly intervention, but this is different. This is one of those times when God shows up and shows off.

It happened when Ed and I were visiting my son Kody, and his wife and daughter. My middle son Kerry, and his wife and two sons were also visiting.

We laughed watching my three old grandaughter Stephanie dance with her black and white border collie that she had named Cousin Twiggy. Stephanies's cat was the same colors as the dog and seemed to think she was also a cousin and was trying to join in the fun.

Later that night we had to figure out where everyone could bed down in their small two bedroom home. Out came the air mattresses. I however chose to sleep on the living room couch.

I normally wouldn't tell anyone that I have false teeth, but I must confess that I do in order to give glory to God for what He did for me. I always take my teeth out when I go to bed, but I made sure everyone was settled down for the night before I did. I had my overnight bag sitting on the floor beside the couch so I placed them on my bag where I could grab them quickly if anyone came in.

I am a light sleeper so as soon as I heard someone stirring around in one of the bedrooms I sat up and reached for my teeth but they weren't there. I frantically got up, lifted the bag, looked all around, even under the couch, and in my blankets, as well as dumping the contents of my bag out and sorting through it.

By then my son came in and asked what I was looking for. When I showed him where I had left my teeth he joined in the search, lifting up the couch cushions, shaking the blankets and looking all over the small living room. I had not gotten up in the night and neither had anyone else.

Then I remembered Cousin Twiggy and the cat. I recalled a previous Christmas visit where the cat had taken off with an ornament from the tree. Would she or the dog carry off my teeth? They were now my chief suspects, but Stephanie gave them both an alibi. She claimed they had been shut inside her room all night sleeping with her.

"Well they have to be here in the house somewhere," Kody's wife Courtney said as she began looking in the kitchen and bathroom. Soon all nine of us were looking under beds, and coats and all manner of unlikely places.

Now I was totally frustrated which reminded me of my new resolve to never waste my time looking all over for something but to pray and ask God to show me where it was or bring it to where I would see it. So we all agreed in prayer but no one else was willing to give up on the search so we continued to look and look again for over an hour. Kerry even lifted the couch up in the air and took off all the cushions for the third time, for as he said, "They have to be here."

Of course I told them that my personal opinion is that little demons who don't have anything better to do sometimes hide things from us just to get us all riled up, and I refuse to give them that satisfaction. Everyone just looked at me, believing in a more rational explanation without being able to come up with one.

Finally Kerry had lost all patience with the situation and said outloud, "God this is ridiculous—please show us where those teeth are!" and as he spoke his eyes darted towards the couch and he let out a shout. Everyone turned to see what he was shouting about. The teeth were sitting on the couch cushion in plain sight! This time I had nine witnesses to God's miraculous intervention in the little everyday problems of our lives. Can you give me another good explanation? I don't think so.

"Open thy mouth wide and
I will fill it."

Psalms 81:10

# THE PRAYING OVER TIRES

Our Gillette, Wyoming to Valdez, Alaska trip 2009

Just being able to go on our trip to Alaska was a prayer answer in itself and the whole trip up and back was filled with one prayer answer after another. But I want to talk about the tires.

My son Kevin had flown up to Valdez, Alaska to work driving cement truck. So when he heard we were driving up for the summer he called us. "I was wondering if you would consider driving my pick-up to Valdez. I could rent a car dolly for your van and would pay half the gas."

Even though we had planned to go a different route, our plans are always set in Jello, and because we liked the idea of splitting the gas expense, we agreed. This meant we needed to drive to Boise to get his truck. When we arrived Ed took one look at his tires and called Kevin.

"Did you know you really need a set of tires for the trip? There is an actual chunk missing out of one, and you have hardly any tread left on the others."

"I know, but I really can't afford the gas, the car dolly and new tires too. I can't buy them till next payday."

This put us in a dilemma since we couldn't just sit tight for another week, so we did the only thing we knew to do. We prayed. We walked around the pick-up praying for a safe trip, that we would have no flat tires on his truck and would make supernaturally good gas mileage. Then we went ahead and rented the dolly, put our van on it and headed out.

The trip from Boise and up to Valdez was a 2,800 mile jaunt. On a long trip like that it is always good to start out with a good set of tires, especially pulling a load, and considering the frost heaves on the Alcan Highway. Therefore from time to time we reminded the Lord about Kevin's bald tires. "Keep them together all the way to Kevin's," we prayed.

Thus we were a little surprised, when we realized we had a flat tire just outside Whitehorse, in the Yukon Territory. But when we got out to see, we were even more surprised that the flat was not on the truck, which had such bad tires, but on the car dolly his truck was pulling—which had appeared to have excellent tires!

We had to laugh, as we realized we had prayed for Kevin's tires but we had neglected to include the car dolly tires. Fortunately we would not have to pay for it since they were covered in the rental agreement.

So we took it in to the U-Haul dealer and they sent a man out to replace the tire. He noticed the tires on Kevin's truck right away. "Boy, those tires don't look too good. How far do you intend to drive on them?"

"To Valdez, Alaska," Ed replied.

"Valdez!" he exclaimed. Isn't that about 600 miles?"

"Yep! That's about right. But these are prayed over tires. The ones on the car dolly were not."

He just shook his head. "Well, hope you make it," he said doubtfully.

And of course we did! Not only that, but after we arrived, Kevin found someone selling a set of four great tires for his truck for less than the cost of one new one. Our God is awesome!

Those who fear you will be
glad When they see me,
Because I have hoped
In your word
Psalm 119:74

# KEVIN'S HARROWING EXPERIENCE

### Valdez, Alaska 2009

In the year of 2009 it seemed as if our adversary, the devil was out to do away with members of our family. Yet each and every time, God intervened and we saw his hand of protection. Here is one such account:

Our oldest son Kevin had landed a great paying job, working for Harris Sand and Gravel in Valdez, Alaska. It did mean he couldn't be around his family much that summer, but after school got out they flew up from Boise to visit.

So when Kevin got the call that he was to take a semi and lowboy into the Glenallen area and bring back an oversized load, he asked permission to take his son Billy with him. All went well on the 250 mile round trip, until they reached the summit of Thompson Pass coming back.

The summit of Thompson Pass has an elevation of about 2,300 feet. It is part of the Chugach Mountain range north of Valdez. The two lane road winds through the mountains and Keystone Canyon on its way to Valdez. Luckily it was not in winter when the pass can really be treacherous with an average of 551.5 inches of snow each year. Thompson Pass holds a couple Alaskan records. One for the most snowfall during the 1952-1953 season in which 974.5 inches of snow fell, and another record for the most snow in one day, which was 62 inches in1955.

That day however was sunny with no reason for alarm. That is until Kevin went to shift down into a lower gear at the summit and the truck died just as he started on his downward decent. This left him with no brakes.

The truck quickly picked up momentum. Kevin unable to restart the truck, radioed the flag cars of the situation. They in turn radioed ahead for the construction crews to clear the way, letting them know there was a wide load, out of control and barreling down on them.

Kevin repeatedly tried to restart the truck to no avail as they flew around corners. He considered having Billy jump from the truck but they were already going too fast and of course there was the danger of the rear flag car that was trying to keep up might run over him. So they just prayed.

The front flag car got out of the way of the 60 ton load at first opportunity but though the rear flag car was going over 100 MPH Kevin was pulling away. Expecting the worst, a fire truck and ambulance had already been summoned.

As they came to the sharp 180 degree corner Kevin thought, "This is it!" But though the truck and trailer were completely side-ways, and some of the tires rolled off their rims, he managed to keep the truck on the road. The estimate was that he was doing about 120 MPH.

Finally, when he was down on the flats, the truck began slowing down and only then was he was able to restart it. Kevin was still badly shaken and he turned to Billy and asked, "Were you as scared as I was?"

"I don't know Dad—how scared were you?"

"I was ready to start crying, "Kevin said.

"Naw, I wasn't THAT scared, "Billy said, "but you were going awful fast Dad."

We just praise God that Kevin was able to keep it on the road, and we are sure he had a little angelic help.

For he shall give his angels
charge over thee,
to keep thee in all thy ways.
Psalms 91:11

# AMANDA'S WRECK

### Valdez, Alaska 2009

My granddaughter Amanda, fell asleep at the wheel at 3AM on her way home from doing janitorial work at Alyeska Pipeline Terminal and went off into the bay at Allison Point in Valdez, Alaska. It was about a 90 foot descent and very rocky but at least it was low tide.

As she rolled, a boulder crashed through the front windshield shattering it completely and a boulder came through the back window and broke off her head rest, yet Amanda suffered no head or neck injury.

She recalled feeling a warm hand shaking her awake. She looked around dazed as her car filled up with water. She realized she better get out of there before the tide came in. She was able to swim to shore and climb up the rocky embankment.

Once on shore she looked out at her totaled car and saw a big salmon jump through the broken out window into the car. Someone stopped and offered to call an ambulance but Amanda assured them she was alright. She had only a small cut under her eye and a mark from the seatbelt on her neck.

A wrecker was called. When the wrecker pulled the car up out of the water, one of the first things the operator, Pat Gunion saw, was her baseball cap sitting on her seat that said "JESUS SAVES." So true! This is why we need to keep our families and loved ones in our prayers every day.

Moreover as for me,
God forbid that
I should sin against the Lord
in ceasing to pray for you:
I Samuel 12:23

# CONCLUSION

As I close, let me assure you that these prayer testimonies are true. They are also just a small sampling of the prayer answers we have experienced over the years. Since the time I completed this collection I have thought of many others I wish I had included but will now save for another collection, for you see, God never stops answering our prayers. That is, as long as we keep asking them.

"And there are also many other things which Jesus did, the which, if they should be written every one, I suppose that even the world itself could not contain the books that should be written. Amen." John 21:25

# THE GOD I KNOW